'I read *Free Spirit* all in one go as I literally couldn't put it down. Tanya Sarne's courage and resilience are utterly awe-inspiring. You could read no better book than this on the zeitgeist of London and Hollywood in the sixties and seventies and the fashion world of the eighties and nineties.'
— Joanna Lumley

'Wherever it was at, Tanya seemed to be. This is an honest, amusing depiction of life as founder of Ghost, the British fashion brand much loved by women of all shapes and ages. As well as navigating life through the sixties and onwards, here is a story of a woman boss juggling motherhood, marriage, romance and every other thread of life's rich tapestry.'
— Alexandra Shulman

'Inspiring, intelligent, brave, plain spoken and wild, Tanya Sarne's memoir tells the story of a woman who is tirelessly optimistic, brilliantly pragmatic and fiercely true to herself. At once a fighter and a dreamer, she has overcome the challenges her personal and professional life have thrown at her with extraordinary tenacity, humour and grace.'
— Susannah Frankel

'Tanya Sarne's Ghost very quickly became the show that all the girls wanted to do – Kate Moss, Helena Christensen, Naomi Campbell, etc. It was really incredible casting and the girls LOVED the clothes. The party after the show was the "party of the week" – she put a great crowd together and everyone turned up. You just wanted to be part of Tanya's gang because she's magnetic, kind and really funny.'
— Sam McKnight

'If there's a woman out there who doesn't have an old Ghost dress hanging in her wardrobe, can you please tell me exactly what you were wearing in the nineties?'
— Alyson Walsh, fashion writer, @thatsnotmyage

'She just makes clothes that people like to wear.'
— Grace Coddington

'The first time I did music for fashion catwalk shows was in 1996, for London fashion house Ghost. I met Ghost's Tanya Sarne, who at the time was one of London's greatest female fashion entrepreneurs and personalities (Jennifer Saunders would base her *Absolutely Fabulous* character on her). What a truly amazing experience and education; I had never experienced a world like it, truly wild and eccentric. It was such an amazingly exciting time, where music, art and fashion came together in an explosive way.'
— James Lavelle of record label Mo' Wax

FREE
SPIRIT

FREE SPIRIT

A Memoir of an Extraordinary Life

TANYA SARNE

MITCHELL
BEAZLEY

First published in Great Britain in 2023 by Mitchell Beazley, an imprint of
Octopus Publishing Group Ltd
Carmelite House
50 Victoria Embankment
London EC4Y 0DZ
www.octopusbooks.co.uk

An Hachette UK Company
www.hachette.co.uk

Distributed in the US by
Hachette Book Group
1290 Avenue of the Americas
4th and 5th Floors
New York, NY 10104

Distributed in Canada by
Canadian Manda Group
664 Annette St.
Toronto, Ontario, Canada M6S 2C8

ISBN 978-1-78472-846-5

A CIP catalogue record for this book is available from the British Library.

Printed and bound in the UK

1 3 5 7 9 10 8 6 4 2

Contributing Editor: Caro Handley

Publisher: Alison Starling
Design Director: Mel Four
Senior Editor: Pollyanna Poulter
Copy Editor: Jane Selley
Senior Production Manager: Katherine Hockley

Typeset in 12/20pt Plantin MT Pro by Jouve (UK), Milton Keynes

This FSC® label means that materials used for the product
have been responsibly sourced.

To my wonderful family,

who have patiently put up with me over the years.

Contents

A Note From the Author

Memories are just that . . . memories. I am sure the people in my book, and those not in my book, will remember things quite differently, but this is my story and this is how I remember it.

Foreword

'Fuck, Mandy, wake up,' I screamed at my friend, who was lying prone on the sofa. I had been woken up by banging on the front door. It was my boyfriend, Andrew, who had just flown in on Concorde for the opening of Ghost's New York store.

'Bloody hell, what on earth's going on here? You do know you're supposed to be at your shop opening, don't you?' he shouted. 'For God's sake, get yourselves together.'

Mandy on the sofa was muttering, 'Shop opening, shop opening.' A minute later, she sat bolt upright.

At this point in my life, I was very near the edge of a total breakdown, rock bottom, whatever you choose to call it. I was drinking heavily, taking all kinds of substances I shouldn't have gone near, and I was exhausted.

New York was the fifth of our stand-alone stores, following openings in London, Los Angeles and Paris. We also had

15 concessions, soon to be 20, in shops like Selfridges, Harvey Nichols, and Printemps in Paris, not to mention a worldwide wholesale fashion business. I had found myself responsible not only for three collections a year, but also for all the accessories needed for the shops. I was overseeing the design of bags, shoes, hosiery, eyewear, knitwear, quilts, cushions and perfume.

Twenty years earlier, in 1978, I had believed I was unemployable, but to keep a roof over the heads of my two small children, put food on the table and clothes on our backs, I had started a small business. That was all I had wanted, but it had become a monster I could no longer control. Or maybe I was the monster. To miss the opening in New York was unforgivable.

How on earth had it come to this?

With my dad, Jean-Claude, at my wedding, 1969.

Chapter One

Los Angeles

———

'Hey, Tarn, we're getting married tomorrow morning, Chelsea Old Town Hall at eleven thirty.'

I looked at Michael, stunned.

'We're what?'

'Getting married. It's my birthday present to you. Oh, and in the afternoon we're flying to Los Angeles. 20th Century Fox have given me the green light for the *Myra Breckinridge* film.' He grinned and took a mouthful of spaghetti vongole.

I stared at him, lost for words. His sheer cheek was outrageous. The next day was my twenty-fourth birthday, and his gift to me was – himself. He had simply assumed I was going to say yes without even consulting me, leaving me no time to invite my friends and no chance to get a wedding dress.

I hesitated. I would rather have been asked than told, but excitement was bubbling up inside me. Despite his conceit,

I loved him, and the possibility of unknown adventure in glamorous Hollywood was compelling. My heart was racing. It was almost too much to take in.

'Yes. Yes.' I finally managed to get the word out.

Michael smiled back at me. 'In that case, the sooner we finish dinner, the sooner you can go home, tell your parents and pack a suitcase.'

It was January 1969, and we were eating in our favourite restaurant, Arethusa on the King's Road, Chelsea, where a host of celebrities like Michael Caine, Mary Quant and even the odd Beatle could often be spotted. From the dining area on the first floor, one could gaze down at the pageantry on the street below, as people expressed their individuality in outrageous costumes. A kaleidoscope of colours paraded up and down the road, all vying for attention in what was then the epicentre of the swinging sixties.

That night, I rushed home to tell my parents and my beloved grandmother, Ekee, the news. They were all delighted for me, if a little taken aback by the short notice and our plans to leave the country straight after the wedding.

The next morning, I headed to one of my very favourite shops, called Mr Freedom. I'd been in there so often that I'd become good friends with the owner, Tommy Roberts. I told him I was getting married in less than two hours' time, and please could he make me look like a bride. Tommy didn't hesitate. Cooing like a mother hen, he dressed me in a simple long-sleeved A-line cream dress with a gorgeous wide scalloped crocodile belt and a big floppy hat. 'My gift to you, darling,' he said, blowing me a kiss. 'Good luck.'

Clutching at my hat, I jumped into a taxi and made it to Chelsea Old Town Hall just in time. Michael, in a dark suit, with a white carnation in his buttonhole, was waiting for me. We made our vows in front of my parents, Michael's father, Ali, and his brother, David. Michael's friend Stanley took the photos, and as Michael was a newsworthy celebrity and I was good-looking, he had no trouble selling them to all the tabloids.

Our reception – champagne and canapés – was at Mr Chow, the restaurant that Michael's friend Michael Chow had just opened in Knightsbridge. The two Michaels had been flatmates, along with Grace Coddington, who had married Michael Chow in 1968 and was then a junior editor at British *Vogue*.

After kissing everyone a hasty goodbye and promising my parents I would write, I grabbed my suitcase and Michael and I headed to the airport. It had all happened so fast, my heart was pounding. I was happy and excited but nervous and apprehensive too. What lay ahead of me in this new life I was about to start?

At Heathrow, we boarded an enormous plane that I was

Michael and I outside Chelsea Old Town Hall after
getting married, 1969.

convinced would never be able to take off, let alone fly. I'd been on a couple of package holidays to Corsica and Majorca, but this was more than twice the size of anything I'd flown in before. As I peered out of the window, a voice came over the tannoy asking all passengers to disembark. Thankfully, I didn't find out until later that the airline had received an anonymous phone call saying there was a bomb on the plane.

We were shepherded through a small door into a dark, damp aircraft hangar. It was a crush to get in and I looked everywhere for Michael among the throng of passengers and crew, but could find no sign of him. As time passed, my excitement evaporated, and by the time we were told we could reboard, I was cold and miserable and not feeling in the least like a bride. Michael suddenly reappeared, telling me he had bumped into an old acquaintance and they had got chatting. Only later, when I got to know him better, did I suspect that the 'acquaintance' was the pretty air hostess who had shown us to our seats the first time we boarded.

I spent my wedding night staring out of the window at the night sky as the huge metal bird lumbered its way across the Atlantic, while next to me my new husband, having downed several Jack Daniel's, slept peacefully.

I'd known Michael for four years. Before we met, he'd been a pop star, Mike Sarne, briefly famous for several hit songs, including 'Come Outside', recorded with actress Wendy Richard. He'd been introduced to me by a former boyfriend and pursued me relentlessly, showing up at my university digs and later tracking me down to wherever I was working. He had the same lean, blonde good looks as Peter O'Toole, and I suppose I should have been flattered, since he still had girls running up to him in the street, wild with excitement. But his appeal was lost on me. I found him pompous and arrogant and wished he would leave me alone.

When I landed a post-university job as assistant to a literary agent, Michael got me sacked by hanging around my office until my boss became convinced I was passing him the agency's secrets. As an apology, he offered to take me out to dinner and turned up to collect me in his red convertible Rolls-Royce Silver Cloud. Ekee, who lived with us, was convinced he was a prince, come to make me a princess.

One date led to another, but despite Ekee's wholehearted approval, I wasn't sure that Michael was the one for me, until he took me on holiday to Capri in the summer of 1968. With sunshine glistening on the water and Michael at his funniest and most charming, I saw him in a whole new light. We danced and laughed and basked in the sun and I fell in love with him.

After his pop career, he'd set his sights on becoming a

film director. His first film, an 'anti-travelogue' set on the Côte d'Azur, called *Road to St Tropez*, had been followed by a film set in London called *Joanna*. It captured the spirit of the swinging sixties and earned him the front cover of *Time* magazine, which declared it 'a dazzling directorial debut'. This led to 20th Century Fox asking him to direct the film of Gore Vidal's novel *Myra Breckinridge.* Michael's dream was becoming a reality.

Eleven hours after boarding, we disembarked exhausted in Los Angeles and headed for the Chateau Marmont. Known as 'the Castle on Sunset', Chateau Marmont was a grandiose building overlooking Sunset Boulevard. It was impossible to miss because of a huge hoarding with a revolving cowgirl perched high up in front of it.

The Chateau Marmont was built to withstand earthquakes; it had survived several over the years and it would eventually become a Los Angeles Historic-Cultural Monument, but when we arrived, it was at its most decrepit. Run-down and shabby, it was perfect for the musicians, actors, would-be film-makers and artists who hung out there.

Word had reached town that Michael was making a movie, so he was instantly besieged by people wanting to be in his film. The phone rang constantly in our small apartment when he was there, and when he wasn't, he was in endless meetings at the studio with the producers, script writers, casting agents, set designers, costume designers and everyone else involved in pre-production.

Michael was the third director the studio had brought in to make *Myra Breckinridge*, as there had been endless problems between Gore Vidal and the producers. It was a difficult film to make even in late-sixties liberal Hollywood. Ahead of its time, it followed the fortunes of a transgender woman who claimed to be her own widow and who attempted to usurp Hollywood's social order by realigning the sexes. Michael was heavily influenced by New Wave European directors like Antonioni, Godard and Truffaut and wanted to make a surreal movie. Gore Vidal did not agree, and finally he withdrew completely from the project.

While Michael was fighting to make the film he envisaged, I was left in the Chateau. I had expected Hollywood to be glamorous, warm and full of sunshine. Instead, it was dark, cold and raining heavily, and while I was happy that Michael was enjoying the trappings of success, it was a shock to find that suddenly I was a nobody. I wasn't an actress or even a minor celebrity, which meant that I was completely ignored. In the space of a transatlantic flight I had gone from being self-sufficient Tanya Gordon to Mrs Michael Sarne, dependent on her husband and with nothing to do.

Despite the troubling feeling that I'd become invisible, I wrote to my anxious parents and Ekee reassuring them that everything was lovely and I was deliriously happy. The truth was that I didn't know anyone and I could only spend so many hours sitting and reading in the occasional bouts of January sun. I tried going for walks, but it seemed walking on the streets was not something one did in Hollywood. Away from everything familiar, I felt lost and ill at ease, and it didn't help that Michael usually returned late in the evening, exhausted and angry. It certainly wasn't my idea of a honeymoon.

We had been living in the Chateau for about four weeks when Michael told me that his friend Roman Polanski was going to Europe to work on a movie and had asked if we would go and stay with his pregnant wife, Sharon Tate, while he was away, as he didn't like her being alone. Michael thought it was a great idea, but my dormant sense of independence surfaced and I flatly refused. As Michael protested that it would be good for me to have company, I yelled that I was not going to stay in the house of some film star I had never met. I wouldn't be able to relax and would be constantly having to watch my behaviour.

'And while we're on the subject,' I shouted, 'I've had enough of living in this mausoleum of a hotel. I want my own house, my own kitchen and my own life.'

Taken aback by my outburst and perhaps sensing my growing depression, Michael reluctantly acquiesced, and the following day he asked his assistant at the studio to find us a house.

Several places were offered, but Michael, determined to have somewhere fitting his newly elevated status as a Hollywood film director, chose a house in the exclusive, private and hideously expensive Malibu Colony. The Colony was where Hollywood's royalty had their beach homes. I pointed out that we had limited resources and suggested it would be more sensible to buy a simple beach cottage somewhere else, but he rejected that out of hand.

On an overcast late-February morning, we left the Chateau and drove to Malibu, where we were interrogated by the security guard at the entrance to the Colony. After convincing him that we hadn't come to rob the stars who lived there, we were allowed in.

Despite the setting, it wasn't my dream house. However, the huge glass window at one end of the living room, facing the beach and the ocean, more than made up for the tasteless furniture. Watching the rolling surf just yards away, I told myself how lucky I was to be living in one of the most exclusive gated communities in the world.

Our neighbours ranked among Hollywood's finest. Next

door to us lived Sybil Burton (Richard's first wife) and her husband, actor Jordan Christopher. Larry Hagman, then starring in *I Dream of Jeannie* and yet to become J R Ewing in *Dallas*, lived a few houses away. Other homes belonged to wealthy entrepreneurs, film stars and film-makers, but many were second or third homes and so they remained empty for much of the time.

At the back of our house was a small self-contained apartment in which Michael immediately installed two young Mexican girls. They were employed to do the cleaning and look after me, even though I insisted I absolutely did not need looking after.

Although I tried to settle into our new home, the change of location did little to alter my mood. In London, I had always worked and had a busy life. Now I didn't know what to do with myself. Every day I would sit on the beach, drawing pictures and writing – mainly nonsense like this . . .

Earth tell me what you know of those secrets written long ago
Lost in the dust of our lives.
I would be the wisest fool if you could only tell.
Speeding planets playing with my mind
Where do you come from, where do you go?
If I give you the gift of speech, will you tell me what you know?

I was trying to make sense of my confusion and my utter loneliness. I felt out of my depth, and to complicate things even more, I had a sneaking suspicion that I was pregnant.

One day I was sitting on the beach in front of our house when, much to my surprise and delight, our neighbour Sybil approached me. She was friendly and utterly charming; the first real human contact I'd had since arriving in LA. She did her utmost to make me feel welcome and at home, and after that we had the occasional walk on the beach together. It was Sybil who arranged for me to see a local doctor, who confirmed that I was indeed pregnant.

When Michael came home that night and I told him the news, he was over the moon. That same evening, he asked me to go to London. Michael Chow and Grace Coddington were moving out of the flat they had shared with him, and his belongings needed to be packed up. He wanted me to supervise their removal from the flat to the house he had leased for us to live in when we returned to England.

I jumped at the chance, eager to see my family and friends, and a couple of weeks later, I flew back to London. My mother and Ekee were thrilled to have me home, fussing over me and worrying about me doing any physical work. I told them a removal company was doing the moving, not me, but as it turned out, they were right to be concerned. While pushing a cupboard in Michael's bedroom to rescue some papers underneath it, I felt a horrible pain. Hours later, I miscarried.

Whether it was the cupboard or it would have happened anyway, I shall never know, but it was a devastating experience. As I lay in bed recovering, I had to muster the courage to tell Michael, knowing how disappointed he would be. He surprised me by being supportive and understanding, telling me to hurry back so we could try again.

After an emotional parting from my family, I returned to my husband in Los Angeles and the house in the Colony. During my absence, Michael had cemented his friendship with John Phillips, who was composing the soundtrack for *Myra Breckinridge*. A tall, dark, charming man, John had found fame with his group the Mamas & the Papas, writing all their biggest hits, including 'California Dreamin'' and 'Monday, Monday'.

Michael was spending what little free time he had at John's Bel Air house, but I didn't get on with his new best friend, who was heavily into alcohol, drugs and sex, while John had no time for me since I wasn't famous, I wasn't seducible and I didn't take drugs.

Although we saw little of one another, Michael was determined to get me pregnant again as fast as he could. Despite only having one ovary – the other had been removed when I was 11 – I instantly obliged, and was advised by doctors to take things extremely gently to avoid another miscarriage. The Mexican girls were told to keep me in bed for the next three months, and my depression returned. I didn't want them looking after me, I wanted my husband.

Michael, however, was struggling with his movie. Mae West, who he had persuaded to appear in what was to become one of her last films, refused to be on set if another woman had blonde hair like hers. Raquel Welch, the star of the movie, refused to be on set if another woman had the same shade of brown hair that she had. Surrounded by prima donnas, Michael was beside himself, so perhaps it wasn't surprising that when he wasn't on set, he was with John, experimenting with various hallucinogenic drugs.

Once I was allowed to get up and about again, bored out of my wits, I decided to learn Spanish and experiment with cooking. To cook I needed ingredients, so I asked Michael for a car. He came home soon afterwards with a beautiful vintage cream Jaguar. It gave me a sense of freedom as, no longer trapped, I scoured Malibu and its environs for the best food shops. Michael had given me the *Larousse Gastronomique*, which I still consider to be the best cookbook ever written. I learned how to make sauces, and wrote to ask Mum and Ekee for their recipes for crème caramel, plum pudding, and various delicious dishes I remembered from home. As a result, I made wonderful five-course cordon bleu dinners for a husband who rarely came home to sample them. Instead, I ate them and put on lots of weight.

Occasionally Michael would take me out to dinner – we met up with Anthony Newley and Joan Collins, who were both working in LA at the time, and later with Sharon Tate, who by then was heavily pregnant.

Sometimes Michael would come home unexpectedly with new friends. One of these was 32-year-old Jack Nicholson. *Easy Rider* was just about to be released, and Jack was in it alongside Dennis Hopper and Peter Fonda. Although they were the stars and Jack's part was smaller, he claimed – arrogantly but as it turned out correctly – that he was going to be a huge star.

Like almost everyone else Michael brought home, Nicholson took no notice of me. The only ones who were kind to me, apart from Sybil Burton, were British actor and producer Barbara Steele and her husband, screenwriter James Poe, who wrote *Around the World in 80 Days* and *Cat on a Hot Tin Roof.* Barbara and James invited me to visit them whenever I wanted. I often did, and their friendship lives on as one of my good memories.

Sadly, Sybil and Jordan left the house next door to move to New York, leaving their two cats, Sugar and Spice, with me. Much to my dismay, John Phillips rented the house as a weekend home and moved in with his new girlfriend, Geneviève. She had starred in Michael's film *Joanna*, and he had introduced her to John. Now they took up residence and Michael had only yards to go to spend time with his new best friend.

One summer evening, he announced that the musical *Hair* was opening in San Francisco, and we had been invited to the premiere. I was excited. I loved musicals, and I had never been to San Francisco, which I had heard was the most European city in America. We flew from LA and a car was waiting for us at the airport. I wanted to explore the city and the roller-coaster roads I had seen in films, but Michael wanted to visit his friends, celebrity hairdresser Jay Sebring and a well-known actor, who had rented a houseboat for the occasion. We arrived to find Jay and the actor with several young girls, who lay around the boat in various states of undress. We stayed long enough to say hello, and then went straight to our hotel. I told Michael I thought his friends' behaviour was disgusting, but he laughed and said they were just having fun. I was beginning to see my husband in a different light, and I didn't like this side of him.

Hair was not as enjoyable for me as it should have been, since the girls on the houseboat remained on my mind. As the cast belted out the finale, 'Let the Sunshine In', I prayed they were not as young as they had looked, and that they had not been coerced.

Not long after our trip to San Francisco, Michael phoned from the studio to say we were having dinner with John Phillips and Geneviève to celebrate Geneviève's birthday. He told me the restaurant's speciality was lobster, and said please could I look my best. Excited to be going out, I defrizzed my hair, put on some make-up and dressed in my staple Mothercare pregnancy jeans, which I teamed with the beautiful white vintage shirt I kept for best.

The dinner was delicious, but as usual my contributions to the conversation were sidelined, so I channelled my feelings into eating all the food that the others, deep in their self-absorbed exchanges, were only picking at.

On the drive back from the restaurant, John told us that Jay Sebring had said to stop by for a drink at Sharon Tate's house over in Benedict Canyon. Jay was a good friend of Sharon's, and with Roman still filming in Europe and Sharon now eight-and-a-half-months pregnant, he often visited. We debated whether to go, but I said I was tired and needed to go to bed, and John and Geneviève were also eager to get home, so none of us went to Sharon's that night.

The next morning, 9 August, we woke to the unbelievable and shocking news that everyone in the Tate house the evening before had been murdered. Sharon, her unborn baby and Jay had been stabbed and shot, along with Roman's friend Wojciech Frykowski and his girlfriend, coffee heiress Abigail Folger. The sixth victim, 18-year-old Steven Parent, had been gunned down in the driveway. He had arrived to visit his friend, the estate's caretaker, then living in the guest house.

It was incomprehensible. We were stunned. We had met and talked to everyone who was in the house that night, and Michael was good friends with Jay, so there was grief and bewilderment alongside the shock. And we couldn't help thinking that it could have been us. Wojciech and Abigail had gone to stay with Sharon, at Roman's request, when we had turned him down.

Roman, devastated by the loss of his wife and baby, returned to LA immediately and came to stay with us. Two policemen and a bodyguard were constantly with him, rotating in four-hour shifts. No one knew whether they thought Roman was involved in the murders or if he was a target. They stayed for four days, and I spent the whole time in the kitchen, producing endless food for all the policemen and bodyguards.

Even after Roman moved out, the police, unable to find a motive and suspecting everyone, kept a close eye on all of us. LA suddenly seemed like the most dangerous place on earth, and I was terrified. I bought a rope ladder so that I could escape through my bedroom window, and at night, if Michael wasn't there – and he generally wasn't – I would barricade the door of my room with a chest of drawers. Even then, I couldn't sleep. The Hollywood dream had become a nightmare. All I longed for was to go home to London and my family.

With mum and dad, just out of the children's home, 1947.

Chapter Two

Beginnings

I was born in January 1945 in Southgate, a suburb of north London. At the time, the war was still raging, and the threat of German long-range missiles, the V-2 rockets, was terrifying the population. My parents were refugees who met in an air raid shelter in Kensington Gardens in 1943. My mother later told me that she heard her native language, Romanian, echoing across the crowded shelter. Excited, she went in search of the source and found two young men, one of them very handsome, discussing life in the language she was born into. They exchanged stories, and months later she married the handsome one.

My parents were homeless and relying on the kindness of fellow refugees to put them up, so at a few months old, I was deposited in a children's home in the country, where I stayed until I was almost three. I hold this early experience responsible for the independent streak in my character.

My father, Jean-Claude, was born in 1920 in Huşi, in Romania, close to the border of Moldova, to a French mother and a Romanian father who was a government lawyer. After school, he went to study mathematics at the elite École Centrale in Paris until war broke out. Paris surrendered and, being Jewish, my father had to escape with only the clothes he was wearing. On his journey south, he made friends with the remains of a Polish regiment, who dressed him in the uniform of a dead comrade, since civilians were not allowed passage at the time. He managed to leave France, but on arriving in England he was imprisoned as an enemy alien. Luckily his mother happened to have a distant relative who was an MP and who vouched for my father. When it was discovered that he spoke fluent Russian, Romanian, French and English, he was assigned to Reuters News, then desperately in need of educated multilinguals, since they had all been snapped up by British intelligence.

My mother, Daphne, was born in Ploieşti in Romania to a Welsh mother and a Polish-Romanian father. In 1938, she won a competition set by the British Embassy. The prize was a trip to England. Her mother, Jessica, known as Ekee, accompanied her. While they were there, war broke out and they stayed. My mother went to study at the London School of Economics while earning a living by working for the BBC Overseas

Service, and Ekee worked as a secretary for a politician, Sir Harry Brittain, at his home in Sussex.

After the war, my parents decided to make England their home, rather than go to America like many of their refugee friends. My father loved England; he thought it the most democratic country in the world. He was a royalist, and he believed, despite evidence to the contrary, that the king or queen could still step in if Parliament wasn't behaving.

When they came to rescue me from the children's home, we went to stay with friends of theirs, a United Nations diplomat who travelled a great deal, and his wife. Courtesy of the diplomat, we had occasional food treats. His wife told me later that she had found me stroking a ham her husband had brought back from Paris. Rationing didn't end in Britain until 1954, when I was nine years old, so such delicacies were rare.

My father was often away, since Reuters was based in Hertfordshire. My mother continued working for the BBC Overseas Service until 1952, when she went to work for the political weekly *Jewish Observer and Middle East Review* (despite not being Jewish), and she seldom appeared until late in the evening. They loved me, of that I am certain, but their work was all-consuming, so I saw relatively little of them.

After nearly two years with the diplomat and his wife, we moved to another temporary home, with a Romanian concert pianist and her husband, the editor of a literary magazine. My parents, when they were there, slept on sofas in the living room, and I shared a small room with the couple's daughter, Nadia. The house was cold, the bathwater tepid and the food meagre, and I hated the feeling that someone was putting up with us, but my parents told me not to complain and that we were lucky to have a roof over our heads.

Finally, my lovely grandmother, Ekee, came to our rescue. Her husband, from whom she was separated, now lived in Paris with his mistress, and he had sent her enough money to buy a short lease on a large mansion flat on what was then the wrong side of the park in Bayswater. This was to be my home until I got married.

Every morning my mother would drop me at the local state primary school before going off to work, which kept her busy until 8 or 9 pm. I adored my mum, but much of my world revolved round Granny Ekee. She would fetch me from school and we would have tea and toast while *Listen with Mother* was on the radio, which always started with 'Are you sitting comfortably? Then I'll begin.'

Ekee had a beautiful voice, and she would sing me all the old wartime songs, 'The Galloping Major', 'Underneath the Arches', 'Daisy, Daisy' and, of course, 'Clementine', plus lots of Gilbert and Sullivan.

She was the youngest of 13 children. As a girl, she was adventurous and wanted to travel, so she went to work as a secretary for a British petrochemical company in Romania. There she fell in love with my grandfather and married him. She miscarried her first child after her ship was torpedoed in 1916 on a trip to visit her family back in the UK. On this visit she joined the Women's Legion, founded a year earlier by the Marchioness of Londonderry. Around 40,000 women volunteered to help out in the First World War, and Ekee was assigned to the motor transport section. On her return to Romania, she drove an ambulance on the Russian front while looking for her husband. Clearly she found him, since in 1921 my mother was born, followed a couple of years later by my uncle Dennis.

By the time we moved into the flat, Ekee felt she had seen enough of the world, so she rarely went out, other than to collect me from school. She had installed herself in one of the three large reception rooms, in which she put a bed and a sofa. When she wasn't doing housework, cooking, or singing songs to me, she would lie with her feet up on the sofa, smoking and drinking. She smoked about 80 little cigarettes a day, accompanied by two bottles of Guinness.

Being an only child, and with no children in the neighbouring flats, mine was a solitary existence. I lived mainly in my head, constantly daydreaming or, as I got older, playing endless games of patience. I was content and I don't think I felt unhappy, although occasionally I would ask Ekee if I was adopted, and she would laugh and tell me not to be silly.

At the weekends when my mother didn't work, I would climb into her bed for a cuddle. My mother had curly blonde hair and beautiful blue-green eyes. She battled constantly with her weight, which meant that she was round, soft, and warm, and those cuddles with her were the best thing in my world. The worst was when she would take me to Paris to visit her bedridden father. He lived on the Boulevard Haussmann, and from his bed he would shout at everyone in earshot. He had absolutely no interest in me, and my only consolation on these trips was the chocolate eclairs in the patisserie downstairs.

When my father came home, everything revolved around him. He was handsome, resembling the film star James Mason, who he loved to imitate. Given that he had a slight Romanian accent, his imitations fell somewhat short, but that never stopped him. I was a little afraid of him, and in awe of him, but the truth is, I don't think I ever really knew him.

Whenever he came home, my mother would hold a dinner party for him. I loved these social evenings, the chatter, the music and the commotion. My parents' circle of friends included a novelist, a wine merchant, a pianist and an ex-model, Cherry Marshall, who had started one of the first model agencies in the UK and who would come with her activist writer husband. There was also a Russian refugee, Vladimir Raitz, who we knew as Vova. In 1949, he had founded Horizon Holidays, the first company to introduce the British people to package holidays abroad.

Ekee would stay in the kitchen preparing all the food, with me helping. I especially liked peeling the skin off big mushrooms, and desserts never left the kitchen without me having tried and approved them. After each course my mother would wheel the big trolley down the long corridor from the dining room to the kitchen, where Ekee and I would load it up with the next course. After dinner, when the guests were drinking coffee and brandy, I was invited into the drawing room and my parents would ask me to dance for them, as I was taking classes at the Russian School of Classical Ballet. The guests, sensing my shyness, plied me with wine or champagne, after which I readily obliged, although I would have preferred to do imitations of King Kong, a film my mother had taken me to see.

Best of all were the days my Uncle Dennis came to see us. His visits, which took place about once a month, followed a set ritual. He would first of all go and sit with Ekee, and they would talk and smoke while I waited impatiently; then he and I would go to the living room, where there was a big radiogram. We would put on the record of *Carmen Jones*, and I would march around the room to the song 'Stan' Up an' Fight!' and cry when the soldier sang in his prison about the flower being his friend. I fell in love with this musical, and still know it by heart.

After we had listened to the whole of *Carmen Jones*, we would talk. My father, who firmly believed that he was right about everything, never conversed with me, he would only lecture me. But Uncle Dennis was different. He was a scientist, and I would sit agog while he explained to me that when I grew up, I would be able to go to a booth at the end of my street and tell the machine where I wanted to go before being turned into electricity and reassembled at my destination, a notion that both thrilled and terrified me.

At the age of nine, I contracted pneumonia and spent several months off school. To cheer me up, my parents bought me a budgerigar I named Kiki. She became my best friend and I loved her dearly. By the time I went back to school, Kiki would fly to me on my return and sit on my shoulder. She kept me company and would nibble the edge of my book while I was doing my homework.

Shortly before I was due to take the 11-plus exam, I began to feel severe pains on the lower right side of my abdomen. I was taken to hospital, where doctors decided it was appendicitis.

But when the surgeon opened me up, he discovered an inflamed ovary. He took it out and I was warned that I would never be able to have children. When I told my mother, she said, 'Don't talk nonsense.' I chose to believe her and didn't worry about it, and as it turned out, she was right.

Despite this small drama, I managed to pass the 11-plus and was accepted at Godolphin and Latymer in Hammersmith, then a girls' grammar school. Arriving on the first day of term, dressed in my uncomfortable grey uniform, I discovered that I had been put in the C stream. I was outraged, and determined to get into the A stream. I listened and worked hard, and at the end of that year I got top marks in all my exams.

Was I moved up to the A stream? No, I wasn't. I asked my teacher why, and she replied that it was because of my attitude. I had no idea what she meant, but looking back, I think I just didn't fit in. My parents were refugees; I was the first generation to be born in this country and the only girl in the school with the name Tanya. There were lots of Susans, Margarets and Marys, but in the late fifties my name was unusual and strange. Britain certainly wasn't the multicultural country it is today.

After this, I didn't bother too much with academic work, and the attitude I had been labelled with became all too real. I was thrown out of needlework and cookery and was cheeky to the teachers, most of whom insisted I would never amount to anything. I was made to feel like an outsider, and the result was that I isolated myself in a world of daydreams where no one could touch me.

I was on the fringes of several groups but not really a part of any – a pattern that would persist throughout my life. There was a gang of girls who were friendly to me, and one day they said, 'Come with us if you want to see something funny.' I went with them to Hammersmith Tube station, where they pointed out a couple of men who were hanging around and flashing their penises at us. The girls laughed and went to get their train and I went off to catch my bus. I had laughed with them, but in truth I was not sure whether what I'd just seen was funny or disgusting or just plain weird.

The secret I never shared with anyone was that I smoked. I began at 14 in a very small way, but by the time I got to the sixth form and was earning money, I was a proper smoker. I would sometimes take taxis to school because I could smoke in the back without fear of being spotted by a teacher. One girl was caught smoking and wearing white lipstick, which was very fashionable, and she was made to stand on a chair in front of the whole school throughout dinner time as an example to all of us.

I managed to escape this particular punishment, though goodness knows how, but I did get into trouble for my uniform.

We didn't have to buy our summer dresses from the school supplier, and as Ekee was an accomplished machinist, we made all my frocks at home, with me designing and her sewing. These were my first attempts at design, and they didn't go down well at school. Either the neckline was too wide, or the dress was too short or too long, the sleeves too tight or the collar not the right shape. I always had to make modifications, which infuriated me.

My mother loved clothes, and she would take me to the sales at Susan Small, one of the most popular fashion houses of the fifties, famous for their party and evening wear. At these sales, women would fight over a dress or a jacket, whacking each other with their handbags while I watched, fascinated. It was my first taste of a really successful fashion business.

My ballet had come to an abrupt end at the age of 12, when I was told I was not the right shape to be a ballet dancer, but I didn't mind, because what I really loved was tennis. I became a junior member of the Campden Hill Tennis Club, where none of the senior members would deign to play with me, except for one young Australian, who offered me a game. Then early one evening, when everyone else had left, he chased me round the court, caught me and stuck his tongue down my throat. I was 14 years old and I was horrified.

Soon after this, I won the junior tournament and began

Winning a tennis tournament aged 14 (I'm on the right).

playing in under-15 tournaments at other clubs. At 15, I won the London County Council girls' tennis championship on the centre court at The Queen's Club – my finest tennis moment. After that, I was asked by Dan Maskell, who was the Lawn Tennis Association's training manager, and was later to become the BBC's 'voice of tennis', if I would like to try out for the British team. Since the winner of Wimbledon only won a bottle of champagne in those days, I said no thank you. The thought of training for hours every day was not appealing.

When Ekee's lease on our flat ran out, a new 999-year one was offered for £3,000. My parents put themselves in heavy debt to secure it, but it gave us all a much-needed sense of security, and we took in lodgers to help pay off the loan. These were usually students, but there was also a friend of my mother's, a famous pianist called Mindru Katz who had just escaped from Romania. Mindru was very short, and perhaps to make up for this, he loved to show off. One night he crept into my bedroom and told me I would have the greatest experience of my life if I let him get into bed with me. I told him I would scream unless he left my room.

I told my mother, but she either didn't believe me or didn't want to believe me; she said I was imagining things. I knew I was not, and after that, I avoided being anywhere near Mindru.

Holidays were rare, and when we did have them, they were

courtesy of Dad's friend Vova, who was making a big success of Horizon Holidays. Mum and I went to Corsica twice, and once all three of us went to Majorca, where Dad frightened the life out of us by swimming too far out to sea. Fortunately a little fishing boat saw him and rescued him. Did he learn from this experience? No, he did not, since he nearly got us all drowned on another holiday, this time on the Norfolk Broads, a network of rivers and lakes in East Anglia. He had rented a 30-foot sailing boat, since according to him, anyone could sail a boat. We slept and ate on board, and to begin with it was fun. But as we got nearer to the coast, our vessel suddenly changed its leisurely pace and we found ourselves rushing towards the North Sea.

As the wind whipped us along, totally out of control, my mother, seeing a boat moored to one side of us, pushed me, screaming at me to jump. I managed to land on the deck of this craft and looked on, terrified, as the boat with my parents on board gathered speed. It was almost out of sight when a group of men standing on a jetty realized the danger and shouted to Dad to try to steer the boat over to them. For once, he listened, and the men were able to catch hold of the rope and pull it in. Even my father had to concede at that point that currents and tides had powers beyond his control.

By the time I was 15, I had started going out in the holidays and at weekends, to parties and the cinema and other girls' houses. No one at home seemed to mind what I did, my mother and Ekee seldom asked me for details, and although I still felt shy in social situations, I was beginning to realize that there was a big world out there in which I could enjoy myself.

My parents told me absolutely nothing about sex; it was never mentioned at home. Not because they were protective – they weren't, really – I think it was just that no one ever thought to enlighten me, and I didn't like to ask. My only encounters with men had been the attempts of the Australian tennis player and the Romanian pianist, both of whom I had vigorously rebuffed. The girls at school were always giggling about sex and boys, and I had no idea why. So when one of them invited me to a party one Saturday night and I met Marc, an attractive French boy, I decided to sleep with him to find out what all the fuss was about.

Sex with Marc didn't impress me, but at least I now understood all the dirty jokes at school. On the plus side, he turned out to be the most fantastic dancer, and together we jived and cha-cha'd our way through various Soho clubs, such as Club St Germain and Le Kilt, where we won the cha-cha competition.

On Saturdays we sometimes went to watch rugby matches at the French Lycée. Marc's brother was in the team and going out with a girl called Jacqueline Bisset, who would later become a well-known actor, and the four of us would go out to clubs after the match.

I needed to earn some money to fund my club nights and cigarettes, so I was thrilled when I got my first weekend job, working as a waitress in a coffee bar. I soon discovered I was expected to serve the customers, prepare the food and do all the washing-up while the manageress sat with her feet on a table, filing her nails. One late Saturday afternoon, after working my fingers to the bone while she did nothing, I threw a bucket of water and potato peelings at her and walked out.

I went round to Marc's house, and since we had no money, we went busking outside the Everyman Cinema in Hampstead with Marc's friend Andrew Loog Oldham, who would a year or two later, at the age of 19, become the manager of a new band, the Rolling Stones. I was too shy to join in, so I held the hat while the boys strummed and sang.

I looked around for another job and saw an advertisement for waitresses to work at the weekend in the Bridge Club, round the corner from my home. I was just 16 and far too young to work in a club like that, but I thought it was glamorous and fun and it made me feel sophisticated. Not for long. On my first night, the manager accused me of stealing and told me to get into his car since we needed to talk about it. I did what he asked, wanting to stress my innocence, but he started driving, and when I asked where we were going, he didn't answer.

He finally stopped in a field somewhere near Heathrow airport, where he grabbed me. I screamed and fought him off, managed to get out of the car and ran. He chased me, pushed me down on the muddy grass and shoved his penis into my mouth. His semen went down my throat and all over my face. When he had finished, he zipped up, walked over to his car without even glancing back at me, and drove off.

I was in shock. I didn't understand what had just happened. Shaking with cold and feeling nauseous, I wiped my face, got to my feet and tried to brush the mud off my jeans. I had no money and I didn't know where I was, so I walked to the nearest road and managed to hitch a lift back into central London, where I went to see Patsy, a friend from the tennis club who lived close to me. I told her what had happened and asked her if I could get pregnant through swallowing semen. I was terrified of this, so I was hugely relieved when she told me I couldn't. I went home, took a bath and never mentioned it to anyone again. Only later did I discover that the club was a front for some very nasty people, headed by Peter Rachman, the landlord whose name would become a byword for exploitation and intimidation.

It wasn't shame that made me keep quiet, although there was some of that. I just didn't see the point of telling anyone – even if they believed me, what could they do? My way of coping with this, as with other painful incidents, was to push forward without giving myself time to stop and think. I'm grateful for this ability, because it worked for me. I didn't brood on what had happened, and although it was a horrible memory, I don't believe I was traumatized.

Me winning the Rag Queen competition at university, 1966.

Chapter Three

The Big Wide World

———

The day I left school, in the summer of 1963, was one of the happiest of my life, despite the headmistress telling me that I would never amount to anything. A friend of mine came to pick me up in his blue convertible sports car, and as we drove off, I waved goodbye to everyone gathered outside the school gates. Now my life begins, I thought exultantly. And I knew exactly what I wanted to do: I was going to be an actress.

Despite the fact that they wouldn't let me into the drama club at school, I loved the idea of acting, and I had set my sights on getting into RADA. However, my parents were dead set against this; they wanted me to go to university, as they both had. After endless argument and discussion, we arrived at a compromise: I would take a year out to properly consider my options, and then make a decision. I was certain I wouldn't change my mind, and I intended to have a fun year while I waited.

First my mother wanted me to go to Romania with her to visit my father's parents, who had not seen me since I was a baby. It was too dangerous for my father to go, since Romania was under the iron fist of the dictator Nicolae Ceaușescu. As a journalist and 'defector', he would be instantly arrested.

I was more thrilled at the thought of spending time with my mother than I was about visiting Romania. However, this trip was to leave me with indelible memories, on the one hand of an exceptionally beautiful country, and on the other of a cruel and oppressive regime.

Our group was given two guides who spoke English after a fashion, and it was up to them to make sure we didn't go anywhere outside the official tour route, which included the unbelievably beautiful Danube Delta and the mountains of Sinaia, where we stayed in the once magnificent palace of the king, who had been forced to abdicate in 1947 when the communists took over. We also went to Mamaia, which was being developed as a holiday resort. The sea was delicious and the beach perfect, but the ugly hotels lining the front, in which visitors were segregated by nationality, were grim.

At one point I managed to corner the younger, not unattractive guide and cross-examine him about life in Romania. He opened up at first, then suddenly broke down in tears and begged me not to repeat anything he had said, as he could be tortured and imprisoned for talking to me. I promised him our little talk would never go any further.

Although the main reason for this trip was to see my grandparents, they were not allowed into the tourist areas. They had been moved from their beautiful mansion to one room in a house with ten other families, where they remained, impoverished and virtually imprisoned. My grandfather was no longer allowed to work as a lawyer and my grandmother had been forced to give French lessons in order to put food on the table. By bribing a few officials, we were eventually allowed a very brief, heartbreaking visit with them. It was to be another ten years before my father eventually managed to get them out of Romania.

When we got back to England, I decided to try modelling, so I got in touch with Mum's friend Cherry Marshall. In the sixties, becoming a model meant first taking a six-week course, during which you were taught how to walk with books balanced on your head, how to get into a car, take one's gloves off, wear a hat and put on make-up, and a useless set of exercises intended to 'keep one's figure'. After this, you had to get work experience in a fashion house for three months before the agency would represent you to go freelance.

Cherry Marshall agreed to take me on the modelling course, but before I started, I met an Italian film producer,

Franco Cancellieri, in the De Vere Club in Kensington, where I sometimes went with friends. He told me he was making a film with Italian heart-throb Rossano Brazzi, star of *South Pacific* and *Three Coins in the Fountain*, and said I would be perfect to play the part of the young girl in the movie; would I like to come to Rome for a screen test? Wild with excitement, I told Mum, who immediately became suspicious and said she needed to meet this producer before she would agree to my going. Franco was invited to dinner, where he promised that it was all above board and he would look after me. Reluctantly Mum agreed, and off I went to Rome, wearing a big straw hat and feeling very important, even more so when someone at the airport mistook me for Claudia Cardinale, a film star who was impossibly glamorous.

The first day was spent sightseeing and meeting Rossano, who was very charming and who invited me to dinner with him and his wife the following evening.

In those days I tended to live in tight jeans, which I took in myself on the inside seams using Ekee's old Singer sewing machine. I wore them with vintage shirts that I found in flea markets. I only had one – beautiful – dress, bought from Foale and Tuffin. I put on this dress and got into the car waiting for me outside the hotel. When I arrived at Rossano's apartment, we had drinks in the living room, after which he told me it was time to meet his wife. He led me into a bedroom, where, propped up on an array of white satin cushions on the biggest bed I had ever seen, was a very large woman with white hair piled high on her head, surrounded by several white poodles.

At this point, an extremely unattractive young man entered the room. Rossano turned to me and asked politely if I would please make love with the young man in front of them. He explained that it was their pre-dinner entertainment and would give them great pleasure. Stunned and shocked, I backed hastily out of the room.

I was handed to a man in the hallway, who drove me back to my hotel and locked me in my room. The next day I was driven to the airport. I returned home disgusted, depressed and out of love with the idea of being an actress.

When I got back, I took the modelling course, after which I was chosen to star in a three-minute Pathé Pictorial film promoting Cherry Marshall's model agency. The idea was that they could turn an 'ugly duckling' into a swan. The film begins with me walking off the street and into the agency's office. The narrator says, 'Have you ever wondered what goes on inside the head of an awkward lass like this one? She's never heard of such feminine things as poise and charm and elegance. Whatever can glamour grooms do with raw material like this?' After I've balanced a book on my head, had make-up applied and so on, the model parade begins, but there is no sign of me. 'What's happened to our Cinderella?' the narrator continues. 'She can't have made the grade, poor lass. Well she didn't have a scrap of sophistication or *savoir faire.*' Then I emerge in evening dress, perfect hair and make-up. 'But wait,' he says. 'There is our Cinderella, she's not only made it, she's the belle of the ball!'

The film, *Model School in Mayfair*, was shown in cinemas along with Pathé News, and I was delighted with myself. You can still see it on YouTube.

For my work experience, I chose a clothing manufacturer in Great Portland Street, the hub of commercial fashion. I was paid £9 a week, and when not modelling for clients, I had to sew buttons on garments, brush and iron them. I was allowed to sit down for ten minutes in the morning and ten minutes in the afternoon, and lunch was half an hour. Freelance models were brought in to cope with the extra workload during the season, and I made friends with an Australian model, Norma Moriceau, who told me she was earning £25 a week. In later years, Norma became an acclaimed costume designer for the Mad Max films, among others. She convinced me I was a fool to stay, and I agreed, so after just a month, I walked out.

The model agency was not happy, but they did send me to prospective jobs. I was too well endowed on top to be a good clothes-hanger, so the only work I could get was modelling underwear and fur. The photographers generally expected sexual favours; one well-known photographer chased me all round his studio, knocking over everything in his path. What with the underwear, the furs and the photographers, I soon decided modelling really wasn't for me either. My parents were right. I decided I would go to university.

I still had a few months left of my year off, so after that, I had a brief stint assisting the cultural attaché at the Persian Embassy (which hadn't changed its name, even though Persia was now Iran), courtesy of an aristocratic student who was lodging with us and who would later become mayor of Tehran. Tragically, he was one of the first to be executed when the revolution began.

I enjoyed this job, but I was covering for maternity leave so it was soon over. My next job was as a go-go dancer in a coffee bar where I knew the owner. There were several girls, and we took turns to dance in a cage in the middle of the floor while customers enjoyed their drinks. I loved dancing, so I didn't mind performing to the hits of the day: the Beatles' 'Love Me Do', 'Blue Velvet' by Bobby Vinton and 'He's So Fine' by the Chiffons.

Some of the girls went out with the men in the coffee bar, but I never did. I had plenty of offers, including from a TV comedy writer who wanted to be beaten up, a musician who wanted to beat *me* up, and a film director who wanted a threesome. At this point my opinion of men was poor and I was fed up with being propositioned. Were all men like this? I wondered. No, not all. I remember walking in Leicester Square one evening sandwiched between two young actors I had met, Michael Caine and Terence Stamp, who shared a flat. They were too busy arguing about who would be the most famous to be interested in me. As it turned out, they both became huge stars very soon afterwards – Terence had recently made the film *Billy Budd*, for which he got huge acclaim, and Michael Caine had just made *Zulu*, which would shoot him to fame.

These two were enjoying the London party scene with a number of other young actors, among them Peter O'Toole and Tony Booth, who was about to hit TV stardom in the sitcom *Till Death Us Do Part*. Tony swept me off my feet and we had a three-month affair. He was 13 years older than I was and I thought him impossibly glamorous. He had already been married once (he would go on to marry four times) and was the father of two daughters, though I didn't know this at the time.

Many years later I was introduced to Cherie Blair, the most famous of Tony's eight daughters, at a cocktail party. I mentioned that I had known her father and she replied, 'You and a hundred others,' before turning away. It can't have been easy for her.

When the go-go dancing became tedious, I went to work as a croupier. I was good with cards due to my hours of playing patience, and I knew Jim, the manager of a small club in Queens Gate called Blaises. It was the forerunner of clubs like the Revolution and the Speakeasy, and although it was primarily a music, drinking and dance club, it also had a couple of gaming tables and Jim offered me a job on the blackjack table.

In my first week, one of the players got desperate when he lost all his money. He told me his wife would leave him and his children would go hungry. I begged the manager to give him back the money he had lost. He smiled and said, 'OK, do that and see what happens.' So I gave the man back his money and told him to go home. He went straight to the roulette table and lost it all over again. I learned a lesson about gambling addiction that night.

Courtesy of all these jobs, I managed to make enough money to rent a television for Ekee, which she loved, and to give her £5 a week for her cigarettes and Guinness. I felt very proud of myself.

Towards the end of my gap year, I met an actor named Ian, who was the first considerate and kind lover I had known and who redeemed, to some extent, my low opinion of men. Many years later, I saw his name in an article and sent him an email asking if he was the man I had known when I was 19. I received the loveliest reply.

> Yes, it is me, the very man! You were Tania Gordon and the sexiest 19-year-old imaginable. I was on the Central Line going to meet Robert Stigwood [then an agent and music entrepreneur, later a film producer] and supposed to get off at Marble Arch, and then I saw you and vowed to stay on the train, get off whenever you did, throw myself at your feet and beg your indulgence. I did, you alighted at Bayswater and then we had coffee and that was that! You ruined other women for me for a very long time. And of course, through me you met none other than the father-to-be of your children. You have led an extraordinary life and today you are Tanya Sarne. A corner of my heart still belongs to Tania Gordon.
>
> Love, Ian

In the autumn of 1964, I started at the University of Sussex, in Brighton. It had received a Royal Charter in 1960 and was considered one of the trendiest universities. My A levels had not been great, and I believe my acceptance was helped by a very old Romanian friend of my mother's who happened to be a professor there.

I set off with a case full of new clothes, bought with my

A picture of me taken by Michael Sarne, 1965.

Sitting on the university sign. Photo taken by Michael Sarne.

gap-year wages, in my father's Ford Zephyr. I had passed my driving test, and since my father was spending most of his time in West Africa setting up radio stations for Reuters, I had the use of his car.

The student accommodation on campus was still under construction, so first-year students were all housed in guest houses in Kemptown, close to the beach. I was put in a room with Carol, a nice girl, with whom I had absolutely nothing in common. All the students in my house played the Beatles endlessly, while I was heavily into soul music: James Brown, Nina Simone and Aretha Franklin. I felt out of place and out of sorts and decided to leave – but then I met Max. He came from Blackpool and was tall with jet-black hair. His father made cheese, his mother was a vegan, and he was wild.

With Max's encouragement, I changed my course from history and economics to history and social psychology, although in that first year neither of us did much studying. Our main problem was lack of privacy, since we were both in shared rooms. When we wanted to have sex, we either went to his room and locked his room-mate out, or to my room and locked Carol out. If she came back, she either had to wait outside or go to another girl's room.

Before the end of the first year, Carol committed suicide. I have carried the guilt for this throughout my life, despite reasoning with myself that I was always kind to her and that her problems must have been much more far-reaching than just being locked out of her room occasionally. It was incredibly sad.

At the end of my first year, I entered the competition for Rag Queen, and won. The prize was a clothes voucher for £50 and an audition to sing with a band. My singing was dreadful, so I wasn't signed, but I happily bought a beautiful mustard-coloured suit from Jaeger, which I still have today.

In my second year, I rented a house. Max and I had the largest room and I let the rest to other students and made a small profit – my first venture as an entrepreneur, although at that stage I had never heard the word.

I did even less studying in my second year, but I did play tennis for the university, and Virginia Wade, who was in her third year, gave me her racquets when she left. (She went on to win the Wimbledon women's singles title and to become number two in the world rankings.) Towards the end of that year, I received a letter from my course tutor issuing a final warning: if I didn't pull my socks up, I was out.

In the summer holiday, I went back to work in Blaises. Max came with me and got a job as a doorman, and between us we managed to save £1,000, which we used to buy a boat, moored in Shoreham Harbour. It had been used in the war to carry troops, so it was spacious, and we were able to take in three students for bed and board. But by the end of the first term, the charm of living on a boat was wearing a little thin, added to which Max was becoming increasingly odd. Small out-of-character incidents culminated on the day I returned to the boat laden with shopping to find all my clothes floating in the water. As I stood there stunned, one of the other students ran past me shouting, 'Watch out, Tanya!' What the hell was going on? Had Max gone mad?

It seemed he had. Before throwing my clothes into the water, he had somehow managed to make a hole in the bottom of the boat, through which water was pouring in. I rescued what I could, got into my car and checked into a cheap hotel. The next day we were both summoned to the dean's office and given a choice: either leave the university or move into the student halls on campus. I chose to move into the women's hall of residence, and Max chose to leave. He was highly intelligent and creative, so I wasn't surprised to hear later that he had become editor of an early Richard Branson venture, a magazine called – ironically – *Student*, which featured stories by John Le Carré, cartoons by Gerald Scarfe, and articles by people like John Lennon, Mick Jagger and James Cameron.

I adapted to my new circumstances with only a few moans and groans, and soon found a new boyfriend. John was the son of a Rutland pig farmer and was emotionally and physically the opposite of Max. Tall and fair, he was a calming influence on me, and I was the missing excitement in his life.

Occasionally my routine was interrupted by a visit from a man my actor ex-boyfriend Ian had introduced me to before I left for university. Michael Sarne seemed to have a real thing about me and would not give up. I didn't particularly like him, and never gave him any kind of encouragement, but despite my coolness, he persevered.

Time flew by, and suddenly I realized finals were fast approaching and I was totally unprepared. I got my head down and began studying as I had never studied before. Various forms of pep pill were readily available, and I took lots so that I could study day and night. My thesis, which Mum typed up for me, was on 'The Intervention of the Executive in the Parliaments of the Cromwellian Protectorate', and I was very proud of it.

Exams followed, but by the time I got to my final history exam, my hands were shaking so violently I couldn't even write my name. I was taken to the medical centre and pumped full of Valium until I normalized, and was then allowed to take the exam later, on my own.

Miracle of miracles, I got a degree. Admittedly it was only a third, but a third was as rare as a first, and I was very happy with it. Back I went to London and home, dreaming of exciting possibilities. It was 1967, the summer of love, flower power and hallucinogenic drugs. John went off to Africa to be the journalist he'd always wanted to be, but I had no idea what I wanted to do. I couldn't sing – something I'd love to have done – and I didn't want to model or deal cards. What else was there?

I answered a small ad looking for female racing drivers. This really appealed to me, because I loved driving. Alex, the man who answered my call, sounded very posh and he arranged to meet me the following day in a local coffee bar. I told my friend Patsy I was going to be a racing driver, and she told me I was naive and vulnerable and to be careful.

Alex arrived in a tweed suit with a cap on his head, and a walking stick. He told me the race training would come later, but first he needed to be sure of my driving skills. He said he would pick me up the following Monday along with three other would-be racers and take us to a car auction. We would each have to drive a car back to our homes, advertise it for sale as if it was our own, and then we could keep ten per cent of what we sold it for.

I sold plenty of old bangers that winter, but the racing training never materialized, and when Alex took me to collect a car in France and then leapt on me in a quiet country lane,

I was furious. Not again, I thought, pushing him off with some difficulty. I got out of the car, hitch-hiked back to the hotel and phoned Mum to wire me the money to get home.

I had another small income, earning £3 a time to read new books and scripts for Universal Pictures. I had to write a synopsis of each and say whether I thought it would make a good film or not. This was a useful extra, but I needed to earn more. Once again I scoured newspapers and magazines, and this time spotted an advertisement from a film, television and theatrical company looking for an assistant for their literary agent. I got the job. My boss was married to the film director Silvio Narizzano, best known for the film *Georgy Girl*, and I was in awe. But despite my excitement and eagerness to please, I failed miserably. Try as I might, I wasn't subservient enough. I also had opinions that were not welcome and forgot to post important letters, which seemed to fall behind a filing cabinet. And then Michael Sarne turned up and lost me the job.

Two years later, I was married to him, living in Los Angeles, pregnant, lonely and wondering where my life was going.

Me and Claudia, 1972.

Chapter Four

Babies

In the last few months of my pregnancy, I experienced a flood of emotions I had never felt before. Jealousy, rage and confusion welled up inside me and I lost my self-confidence. I loved my husband deeply, and knew he loved me, but Hollywood had changed him.

His film was finally finished, after endless rows and problems during its making. Michael had been happy with it, but when studio head Darryl F Zanuck saw the final edit, he insisted that several scenes be taken out, after which Michael felt it was no longer the film he wanted it to be.

He was restless and moody, and he had taken to going out every night, without telling me or letting me know where he was going. Often he didn't return until dawn. When I asked him where he had been, he told me he was at John Phillips's house working on a script idea. I wasn't a complete fool; I knew they were drinking and taking drugs together and that little if any work was being done.

I was also fairly sure that Michael was seeing other women. Our sex life had vanished with my pregnancy, as Michael didn't think the two went together. Added to which I had been stuffing myself with the food I cooked for him that he barely ever turned up to eat, so I had put on several stone.

My loneliness and isolation often led me to write. This passage I wrote at the time sums up the absolute misery I felt:

The door slammed shut. I rushed downstairs, but too late. The car was already pulling out of the driveway. I called him all the names under the sun until I had exhausted myself. I went into the kitchen to make a cup of tea. This always had the effect of calming me down for at least a few minutes. There had been no row. There never was, but a growing restlessness and then he was gone. Maybe he just needed some air and would be back in a few minutes? Who was I trying to kid? He had gone to pick up a girl somewhere and then sleep with her. The kettle was boiling. I squished the tea bag round in the cup and added lots of sugar. What was the point of dieting? Nobody wanted me anyway. How about some toast and honey? Why not. There was nothing else to do. I went upstairs with my little feast, quickly undressed, put on my cosiest nightie and climbed into bed. Suddenly the roar of an engine made me sit bolt upright. Maybe it was him. But no, the car had driven past.

As 1970 dawned, my due date drew near and Mum flew out to be with me. The day after my birthday, close to midnight, my waters broke. I didn't know what to do. Mum had gone to bed, and I didn't want to wake her because I was embarrassed that Michael wasn't home and I had no idea where he was. Besides which, the hospital was almost an hour's drive away, and Mum didn't drive.

I phoned John Phillips's house. There was no answer. I grabbed the phone directory and started calling every restaurant and club where I thought Michael might be. He wasn't in any of them, and with my contractions becoming stronger, I began to feel desperate and very frightened.

He finally arrived with daylight. Telling me not to get so worked up, he piled me into the car and drove me to Cedars-Sinai hospital. When I walked in, the midwives were convinced the birth was some way off, but half an hour after I arrived, my baby made an appearance. My blood pressure was sky high, but thankfully our baby girl, born on 17 January, was quite normal.

Michael had asked Mae West to be the baby's godmother,

and she had graciously accepted. While I was still in hospital, she phoned to ask what colour the baby's eyes were. I told her they were blue. 'Oh my! That's wonderful, dear,' she said. I never heard from her again, and neither did her godchild.

Michael fancied Claudia Cardinale, the actress I had been mistaken for on my ill-fated trip to Rome, and I liked the name, so Claudia it was. She was a beautiful baby, and Mum and I, and occasionally Michael, doted on her, cooing and kissing her and singing her songs.

A couple of weeks after we came home, Mum returned to London and her work, leaving me with the Mexican girls and Michael, who continued to be absent most of the time. The dreadful early reviews for his film had thrown his future career into doubt. I knew he was suffering and felt desperately sorry for him, but I was suffering too. One night I completely lost it. Leaving my four-week-old baby with the Mexican girls, I set off to look for him, turning up at every smart Hollywood restaurant, until I finally found him having dinner with a pretty young hairdresser. I made a complete fool of myself shouting and screaming at him, but I was beyond caring.

I now know that one can't change another person. One either accepts who they are or leaves. But I didn't know that then, and I hoped that somehow Michael would come back to me and Claudia and we could be a family together.

That night when we got home, Claudia, thankfully, was sleeping soundly. I was still very distressed and Michael insisted on giving me a pill to calm me down. I don't know what it was, probably some kind of sedative, but I was unused to drugs of any kind and I fell into a sleepy trance while sitting on a chair. When I came to, the first thing I saw was hair on the floor all around me. *My* hair. I put my hand up to my head and felt only short tufts.

'What have you done?' I gasped.

Coolly he told me that I was too fat, and that he'd cut my hair off so that, without my pretty curls framing my face, I might be encouraged to lose weight. I didn't know if I would ever forgive him. I understood by then, having met his father, who had brought Michael and his brother up after winning custody from their mother, that Michael had inherited more than a touch of misogyny. But this was too much.

The next day I went out and bought two wigs, which I hid under until my hair grew back.

Furious as I was with him, I knew he was right about my weight, and I put myself on a strict diet of raw carrots, raisins and almonds until I got back to my previous size.

Unlikely to be offered another film in Hollywood after the reviews, Michael announced that he was going to Rome, where he would write his own script. He hoped the booming

Italian film industry might be a little kinder to him. He took off, leaving me with a six-week-old baby, no money, some valuable art he had acquired, the phone number of his lawyer, and a long list of people he owed money to. He told me not to worry, since the lawyer would take care of everything.

A couple of days later, his Mustang convertible was towed away for non-payment. I hoped my old Jaguar had been paid for, because I needed a car; it was impossible even to get to a supermarket without one. I phoned the lawyer, who agreed to meet me the following week.

When Claudia was sleeping, I left her in the care of the Mexican girls and went for long walks on the beach, where the sea air and the sound of the waves calmed my fears and apprehension. On one of these walks I bumped into a neighbour of ours, French film director and producer Roger Vadim, who I had met previously with Michael. He had been married to Brigitte Bardot, with whom I suspected Michael had had an affair before we were together. Roger was now married to Jane Fonda, but their marriage was on the rocks. He told me I was the first woman he had been attracted to since he met Jane, and that did my battered self-esteem a world of good. We began an affair that was a brief, if lovely, diversion from my problems.

When I met the lawyer, Jack, he told me that Michael owed $20,000 and that there were no funds in America. He suggested he take all the art Michael had bought as security, settle the debts, pay off the Mexican girls and buy me a ticket back to London. He would also give me enough money to live on and get a passport for Claudia. I had no choice but to say yes, although the art he wanted included an original Marilyn by Warhol, a Fontana, and 12 Warhol lithographs of the Kennedy assassination that Michael had given me as a present. Neither of us ever saw these priceless pieces again.

With Claudia in my arms, I left LA with no regrets. It really wasn't a friendly place unless one was famous or rich. I missed seeing people walking in the street. I missed Mum and Ekee and familiar surroundings. I was longing to get home.

Before we had left London, Michael and I had gone house-hunting and it had come down to a choice between two properties. One was a lovely freehold house with a studio at the back on Ladbroke Grove for sale at £20,000. The other was a grand old Victorian terraced house in Kensington, with five floors including a spacious basement where the very large kitchen was situated. This house had its own lift and it was available on an 11-year lease for £11,000. No prizes for guessing my choice, but Michael wanted the Kensington house. It was no use my telling him it was much more sensible to buy a freehold. He wanted the house with the lift, so that was the one he bought.

This was where I had moved the furniture from Michael's flat, but we had never actually lived in it, and when I moved in with Claudia after our return, it presented problems that would have confounded the best of housewives, of which I was not one. For a start, it was only partly furnished, and there were no curtains or rugs. We did have a bed in the main bedroom, which overlooked beautiful communal gardens, but the kitchen was three floors down and I had to take Claudia with me just to make a cup of tea. The lift made me nervous, so I preferred to take the stairs, which were icy cold – the whole house was freezing.

The only means of cooking in the kitchen was on an old coal-fired Aga. Coal had to be ordered and delivered through a hatch in the pavement into the cellar underneath, where I had to collect it, coal scuttle in hand, before trying to fire up the Aga. It took an age to get it hot enough to cook anything, and even then it was painfully slow; a tiny chicken took at least five hours.

The house was an impossible place in which to live on one's own with a baby, so my parents lent me some money and I found a young au pair to move in and help me. I still had an account at Harrods, which Michael had set up for me before we left London and which I kept alive by visiting the chairman, Sir Hugh Fraser, for tea once a month. We had met when I demanded to see him to explain why I couldn't pay my account at the end of every month. I would flirt with him, and he enjoyed my visits, so the account was not closed. If only I could have dealt so easily with all the other debts piling up. Michael had sent most of his fee for the film to his brother, David, to pay off his debts and invest the remainder. I contacted David and he arranged a Diners Club credit card for me. In this way I managed, but every day was a challenge.

I hadn't heard from Michael in weeks. I knew he had an apartment near the Spanish Steps in Rome, and I had also heard from various acquaintances that he was having an affair with an Italian actress, Monica Vitti, who had worked with one of his idols, Antonioni. Finally he phoned me to say that he was going back to Los Angeles to discuss an idea for a film he and John Phillips had dreamed up. Would I please go to Rome and pick up his red Rolls-Royce convertible and drive it back to London.

I loved driving his car and welcomed a change and a little excitement, so a few days later, I boarded a train heading for Rome, via Paris, with Claudia and the au pair. But as the train pulled into Paris, the au pair said she wasn't well. She left us and I didn't hear from her again.

Claudia and I arrived in the beautiful city of Rome, and after dropping our suitcase at the hotel, we set off for a walk along the Via Sistina. Suddenly a group of young men armed with cameras gathered around us, and I realized too late that it was my handbag they wanted, and not a photograph. I had both arms wrapped around my baby, so I couldn't stop them running off with it. I was left with no passport, no money and no credit card.

The hotel manager was very helpful, and after phoning Diners Club to stop my stolen card, he arranged for me to be driven to where Michael had left his car. At least I now had transport. The British Embassy was the next stop. While I was waiting, I started chatting to a young man, a dancer, who'd had a similar experience: all his possessions had been stolen, and he had to get back to London. The embassy was helpful with papers and a temporary passport, but very mean on the money side, and I guessed it would be the same for the young man, so I invited him to join us in the car back to London. Expenses would be halved, and I would have help with my daughter. He was delighted, and we had a really fun trip. He kept Claudia amused with all sorts of funny faces, and I had someone to talk to.

No sooner had I got back to London than Michael called to say would Claudia and I please join him in Los Angeles, where he was staying with John and Geneviève in Bel Air. He said he and John were developing their idea for a film about Lord

Byron and Percy Shelley, and there would be parts in it for me and Geneviève.

I didn't want to stay with John and Geneviève, and the film idea sounded like the result of Michael and John getting carried away during one too many late nights, but I did want to be with my husband, and if there was a chance I could finally be an actress, I wanted that too. I phoned Michael's brother, who was apparently organizing my ticket. David was an actor who hadn't worked in a long time, but when I went round to see him, I noticed that his formerly shabby flat was now full of new furniture and an up-to-the-minute sound system. Was this how he'd invested Michael's money? I wondered. I said nothing.

Mum and Ekee were not happy. They said it was too much travelling and we needed to stay in one place and make a proper home. This was no way to live, they insisted. I agreed with them, but I had married a man who seemed to be constantly on the move. What was I to do? We said a tearful goodbye, and with Claudia in my arms, I set off once more for Los Angeles.

Michael met us at the airport and the three of us had a joyful reunion. It was wonderful to be with him again, and all the trauma and infidelity of the past were forgotten – until we arrived at John's home. I was excited about seeing my lovely old Jaguar, which John had been asked to look after. I glanced around but couldn't see it. John told me that it was at his manager's house, and I wondered if I would ever see it again.

After I had fed Claudia and put her to bed, I sat down with Michael and John to ask how the film was going. It seemed that, high on acid or mescaline, they had decided they were Byron and Shelley reincarnated. John wasn't keen on me getting involved, and for once I agreed with him. In the following days, they approached several studios, but got nowhere. Darryl F Zanuck gave them short shrift.

After less than a month, the three of us flew back to England. It was autumn 1970, and my joy at returning to the safe haven of London and our house was somewhat dampened by the discovery that our electricity was about to be cut off. Along with plenty of other overdue bills, there was also a letter from the bank manager. As we soon discovered, Michael's financial affairs had been totally mismanaged by his brother. We were broke, but Michael lived with his head in the clouds and didn't seem to be too troubled by any of this. He told me to go on using my Harrods account and he would sort it out. Perhaps he did, because for a few months, life was fairly peaceful.

Almost every day I would take Claudia to nearby Holland Park and then to visit her grandmother and great-grandmother, both of whom doted on her. Ekee would spin coins in front of her; Claudia loved watching them clinking and would gurgle with delight.

Michael had moved his father to a flat within walking distance of our house and would visit him most days. He was restless, and in the aftermath of his rejection by Hollywood, his alcohol consumption had increased.

Soon after Claudia's first birthday, in January 1971, he rented a chalet in Château-d'Oex in Switzerland for three months so that we could learn to ski. I was happy that we were going to spend some real time together away from his drinking pals in London. The chalet was lovely, and we found an excellent little nursery in the village for Claudia while we were on the slopes. We learned quickly, and after skiing each day we ate in one of the little restaurants high on the mountain, where the delights of fondue and red wine still linger in my mind. In the village I bought lovely fresh local food, and for the first time Michael was eating the dinners I cooked.

My peace was short-lived. Two months into our stay, Michael came back from the village bar one evening with a strange woman. I wasn't sure whether he planned to sleep with her or for us to have a threesome, but whatever it was, I wasn't having it. I locked myself in a bedroom and the next day I left with Claudia.

My father was visiting his aunt in Digne in France,

intending to come and see us next. I phoned him and we met halfway. He wasn't at all sympathetic. He told me I had made my bed and I had to lie in it, and persuaded me to return to Michael. I did, but the damage had been done. Our skiing adventure came to an end and we returned to London.

I'd hoped that Michael had sorted out our financial problems, but after our return, court summonses from our creditors started to arrive again, many of them addressed to me. I became frightened to answer the door in case it was another summons or a bailiff.

Michael never seemed in the least concerned. These 'little things', as he called them, never worried him. He had several sketches and tapestries by pop artist Roy Lichtenstein, which he had commissioned for his swinging sixties film, *Joanna*, and he sold one or two, which helped us in the short term.

In the autumn, I found I was pregnant again. Michael was thrilled – he wanted lots of children – but only weeks later, he told me he had finished a script he'd been working on, based on *Don Quixote*, the Spanish novel by Cervantes, which he had transported to Manhattan's Bowery district, where all the drunks hung out. He was off to New York to set up finance for it.

Here we go again, I thought. I couldn't have stopped him, nor would I have wanted to. And to make matters worse, he had asked his father to keep an eye on me. After Michael left, whenever I turned around, there he was. He had a key and would let himself in, which upset and unsettled me. He seemed to enjoy spying on me.

Two months later, Michael called to say that the film was ready to go. He had booked us rooms at the Hotel Navarro on Central Park South and I should come as soon as possible. I was happy at the prospect of being reunited with Michael and curious to see New York, so I packed us up and off we went.

When we arrived, he told me the actors for his film, including his star, John Carradine, were on their way, but I thought it strange that he had just one assistant and no office. Still, what did I know about making films? I left him to it, and Claudia and I explored the city and walked in Central Park, where we would stare at the animals in the mini zoo, coming back with icicles hanging off our noses.

One day we returned from the park and couldn't get into our hotel room. I went to reception and was told we had been locked out for non-payment. Help! Where was Michael? After some hours, he finally appeared to tell us that the finance for the film had fallen through, but an acquaintance of his had an apartment on the other side of the park where we could stay for a nominal rent, to be paid later.

It was a smart address on Park Avenue with a uniformed

doorman in attendance, but my hopes turned to horror once we got in. The place was filthy and had clearly been neglected for a long time. There were cockroaches everywhere. We had to sleep on top of the beds in our clothes until I could wash the bedding and hoover the mattresses.

We spent a sad Christmas and New Year in the apartment. The mood changed early in February, when Michael announced that he had done a deal, and the film could now go ahead.

In March, however, came the news that my lovely Granny Ekee had died. I was devastated. Claudia and I returned to London for her funeral and stayed with Mum, but it didn't feel the same without Ekee and I don't think Mum ever fully recovered. A year later, my father moved his parents in, after getting them out of Romania, and my French grandmother made my mother's life hell with her endless demands and her insistence on being the centre of attention.

Before Claudia and I flew back to New York, I checked with Michael to make sure the film was still going ahead. He said it was, so, now heavily pregnant, I resumed my repetitive life of eating, sleeping and taking Claudia to Central Park, where on occasion we would find a dead body. New York was a wild and dangerous place in the early seventies.

Once again, however, the finance deal fell through. Refusing to give up, Michael continued to hustle his way through every conceivable avenue, while our money situation became steadily worse and my due date approached.

In late May, Mum flew out to be with us. She filled our bare fridge, which made me feel more secure. This time Michael was there when my waters broke. We walked together hand in hand to Lennox Hill Hospital, a couple of blocks away, and he stayed with me throughout the birth, which, thankfully, was straightforward. We called our son William.

Kissing us goodbye, Michael promised to come back the next day to take us home and pay the bill. I waited and waited, but no Michael. That night, I picked William up, cradled him under a blanket and left the hospital via the external fire exit stairs. I walked home to Mum, who looked after us for the next three weeks. I have no idea what I would have done without her.

The day after she left, we received a court summons for non-payment of rent. My understanding was that the owner of the apartment had agreed to wait until we had money, but this turned out not to be the case. I didn't want the police coming round, so on the specified date, Claudia and I went to court, leaving William with Michael.

The court wasn't at all like a courtroom in England; it was noisy and crowded with people waiting to come before the judge.

'Why haven't you paid your rent?' the judge asked me when my turn finally came. I replied, not entirely untruthfully, 'I just gave birth to my new baby three weeks ago, and my husband hasn't been home.' To which he replied, 'Well what are you doing here? Go home and look after your baby.' I did just that, feeling as if I was walking on air, I was so relieved.

That night I told Michael we had to have a serious talk. I tried to keep the hysteria out of my voice as I told him it was impossible to continue living in New York. At least in London we had a house, and I had my parents, who would help out in an emergency. For once he agreed with me, and as soon as we had a passport for William, we left.

Back in London, a pile of final demands greeted us. It was hopeless trying to talk to Michael about money. He would just shrug it off and tell me not to worry. But I did worry. I ordered coal to get the Aga going and borrowed money from Mum to buy food. The children's room had no furniture, so they slept with us. When I went out, I left by the basement door in case there was a bailiff outside or someone trying to serve a warrant.

Determined to use the Aga to my advantage, I read in my *Larousse Gastronomique* about a cassoulet that had been kept going for 30 years. Perfect! I bought the cheapest cuts of meat, and any bones the butcher could throw in, used the biggest pot I could find, added beans and vegetables, and put it in the

Aga. After many hours, we had a wonderful cassoulet. I added to it every two days and it worked brilliantly. Michael would eat whenever he came home, baby William had the soup, and Claudia and I had one meal a day from it, eating scrambled eggs or omelette for our other meals.

Michael, who had decided to get a band together, spent most of his time hanging around the house drinking with out-of-work musicians. I still loved his eccentricity, his warmth and his wit, but his lack of common sense was driving me mad. And I was restless. I couldn't help feeling there had to be more to life than looking after small children and struggling to make ends meet.

Weeks later, he announced that he was going to Brazil. He had been reading Gabriel García Márquez's novel *One Hundred Years of Solitude*, and he said the Brazilian TV company Globo was interested in him and his work. He would send for me and the children as soon as he had a home for us. Early in 1973, he took off, leaving me with two small children, no money, and the wretched Aga.

One of my portfolio photos taken in Brazil by David Drew Zingg, summer 1974.

Chapter Five

Brazil

———

I had no idea where, in one of the largest countries in the world, Michael was or what he was doing. He had been gone for nearly six months, and there was a string of creditors at my door. My life had become one of endless ducking and diving, and I'd had enough.

Michael had left me a credit card, which he said would see us through until he got back. But the card had been stopped after a couple of months. I had managed to avoid the person trying to serve me with a bankruptcy petition, but the pile of bills was growing daily. The Electricity Board had sent me a 'notice of withdrawal of supply', and letters from other creditors were becoming so threatening that I didn't dare open them. I was surviving on my credit at Harrods, but by this time even that account was on thin ice.

With the children to look after, it was impossible for me to find work. William, at a year old, was just about walking, and Claudia, at three, was a handful, albeit a delightful one. My life was becoming one of endless anxiety, and I was exhausted. Did I still have a husband? I needed to find out. Six months apart was long enough. I had to find my arrogant, impulsive, hopeless but lovable husband, and a way out of our mounting debts. Action was needed.

All I had to bargain with were the remaining Lichtenstein artworks. These were rapidly increasing in value, and I hoped I could use them for collateral.

I went to see Michael Chow, Michael's former flatmate, whose restaurant was now one of the trendiest in town. He was busy and didn't want to talk to me, but I kept going back, and in the end my persistence paid off. With a Lichtenstein as security, he lent me enough money to settle all the outstanding bills. After that, I found a friendly art dealer who was looking for somewhere to live – he agreed to move into our house and take care of the bills in lieu of rent. Next I went to the private bank where Michael had an account and gave them the last two Lichtenstein sketches as security for a loan. The money was enough to buy return tickets to Rio de Janeiro and to survive in Brazil for a few months.

I wrote to Michael at the address he had given me and told him we were coming. Would he get my letter? Would he meet us at the airport? I wasn't sure.

It was August 1973 when Claudia, William and I boarded the plane for Rio de Janeiro after an emotional goodbye with my parents. It was difficult trying to keep the children amused and prevent them from bothering the other passengers, and we arrived after the 12-hour flight totally exhausted.

When we stepped off the plane, the heat and humidity were intense. It was like being in a sauna, and I felt as if the earth was swallowing me. Thankfully, Michael had received my letter and was waiting for us in arrivals, where we had a slightly restrained and awkward reunion. He told me he had found a lovely house for us to stay in, two minutes' walk from the beach.

'Lovely,' I said. 'Is it in Rio?'

He was evasive. 'Umm, no, a bit further away.'

I was too tired to ask for more detail. We went to an airport hotel, where the four of us had a much more loving and meaningful reunion in the privacy of our suite, but Michael did not tell me where he was living or what he was doing, and eventually I gave up asking.

The following morning, much revived, we set off. It was only on the way that Michael told me that the house we were going to was in a small seaside town called Amaralina, in the state of Bahia, a thousand miles from Rio.

Why there? Why so far away from the action in Rio de Janeiro, or São Paulo, or even the capital, Brasília? Michael explained that he had made friends with the composer and musician Caetano Veloso, a superstar in Brazil, who had lent us his house in Amaralina. He added that he thought it would be much better for the children to be in a seaside town where they could play on the beach and swim in the sea rather than sweltering in a big city. There seemed no point in mentioning that Rio also had beaches and sea – to stay in Rio would have been expensive, and this was free.

Michael promised he would be there with us and that we would love it. In any case, there was little I could do, although I was worried about the children being cooped up in a car for hours, since it would take us at least two days to get there.

Away from the environs of the airport, the scenery became interesting. We passed field after field of sugar cane. Everyone chewed sugar cane, which explained why so many of the people we passed were toothless, and along with black beans, it was the staple diet for the people who lived in the shacks in the villages we drove through. Small cups of strong black coffee were freely available in the petrol stations; everyone needed a hit of coffee to stay awake in the humidity and heat.

We stopped often to let the children run around, so in the end the journey took us three days. By the end, I had decided I liked Brazil. The people were friendly and the scenery was breathtakingly beautiful.

Amaralina was a pretty town, and our house was small but comfortable. It was in a square, with houses lining both sides of grassy gardens with the beach and sea at one end. It reminded me a little of my first year at university in Brighton, where I had lived in a square off the seafront.

I was happy to be there, and happy to be with my husband again. Life in those first few weeks was idyllic. Claudia, playing with the other children in the square, learned to speak Portuguese in less than three weeks; she became my spokesperson and interpreter.

Every day, the three of us – and sometimes the four of us, when Michael wasn't working on his script – would walk the short distance to the beach. The sea was delicious and the waves were warm. Claudia could swim a little, but I always had to keep a watchful eye on William, who was a bit of a daredevil and would be knocked flying by the waves if he ventured in too far.

From time to time, Michael disappeared. He was into Macumba, an Afro-Brazilian religion bordering on witchcraft, and would go and visit his Mãe Menininha, the spiritual mother of Macumba, for guidance, in much the same way Catholics might see a priest, or New Yorkers a therapist. The difference being that therapists and priests don't cut off chicken's heads, go into trances or perform ritual dances.

Claudia and William in Brazil.

My kids playing with some of the local kids outside our house in Brazil.

We had been in Brazil for five weeks when my skin turned yellow and crinkly, like charred paper, and I developed a fever. Michael took me to the local hospital, but it was filthy; there was blood everywhere and people lay on the floors waiting to be seen. We couldn't get out of there fast enough. Fortunately, one of our neighbours in the square was a doctor. He diagnosed hepatitis, probably caught from water, and told me to stay in bed in a dark room and to eat only soft, bland food. Under no circumstances was I to go out in sunlight or go in the sea.

Michael, however, was convinced that the Macumba goddess of the sea, Yemanja, could cure me. When the sun went down, he carried me to the sea and let the waves splash over me while praying for her help. The salt water was agony on my skin, and I begged him to take me back to bed. Thank goodness for our lovely neighbours, who fed and cared for the children and cooked me all the right foods. They introduced me to papaya, which they said had healing qualities, and I have breakfasted on this wonderful fruit ever since.

Gradually, and almost certainly without the help of Yemanja, I recovered. Soon afterwards, one of the neighbours who had helped me through my illness turned up on the doorstep with a young man. They explained that his name was Edvaldo, and he'd been sold to a family when his own parents could no longer afford to feed him. He had worked hard and faithfully for this family but one day had woken up to find them gone. Now he was destitute. Would I take him in?

Still weak from my illness, I was delighted at the thought of having someone to help around the house, do the shopping, and keep an eye on the children when they were out playing with their friends, so I agreed to give him a home. Edvaldo, who was short of stature and a little slow, got down on his knees to kiss my feet with gratitude. I told him there was no need for this, and with Claudia's help gave him a list of chores to attend to. He became devoted to us, and was a big help with all the household duties and with the children, who grew fond of him. One day he came back from shopping in the market with a baby monkey for William. William was overjoyed and played with the creature all day. Come bedtime, he refused to be parted from it and took it to bed with him. The next morning when he woke up, the monkey was dead. He had slept on the poor little thing and suffocated it. He was inconsolable and cried all day.

We were almost through the money I had brought with me, and I was starting to panic, when Michael told me his deal to make a film with Globo was going ahead, and we would be moving to Rio de Janeiro. This brought a big smile to my face. Although I had experienced genuine kindness and humanity in Amaralina, it was a small provincial town in which I couldn't see a future for any of us, or any way to make a living.

We left after Carnival. This celebration is held all over Brazil just before the beginning of Lent. In Amaralina, everyone locked their front doors for three days and nights and went drinking and dancing in the streets. There was music everywhere, the samba beat unmistakable, as was the stench of urine. I had heard that in Rio it was more of a costume show, but in Amaralina it was a people's carnival, where inhibitions and anxieties were thrown to the wind and everyone lived to dance to the music.

Michael flew back to Rio and rented an apartment with the only credit card we had that was still working. He left me the rented car, and after a very fond farewell with all our neighbours, I set off on the long drive with Edvaldo, the children and our luggage.

Two days later, we arrived in Copacabana, where we found the apartment Michael had rented in a busy street three blocks away from the beach. I would have preferred to be on the more glamorous side of Rio, in Ipanema, but that was beyond our budget.

The apartment was basic, but we settled in. I should have been glad to have Michael at home a lot, since he so often wasn't, but he appeared dispirited and depressed. It seemed the Globo deal was not to be. I decided that if we were going to eat, I had better earn some money.

I found a company looking for tour guides for Americans visiting Brazil. I was accepted, but before I could be let loose on the tourists, I had to do a six-week course on the history of the country. It was a bit like doing my A levels all over again, but much more interesting. I was fascinated to learn that millions of enslaved people had been brought over from Africa to work on the sugar plantations and their descendants now populated Brazil.

I had to wear a uniform, which consisted of a white shirt and an A-line grey skirt with a matching jacket. Once I had shortened the skirt and made a few other minor adjustments to make it more personal, I was ready to stand in front of a busload of Americans with a microphone in my hand and entertain them with my new knowledge. As instructed, I stopped at all the souvenir shops, smiled charmingly at my charges and kept the information coming. I thought I was the perfect guide, until after my third tour, I was called in to head office and told that my services were no longer required. What on earth had I done wrong? Was it that my skirt was too short? Had my groups not spent enough money at the souvenir shops? No reason was forthcoming, so I will never know.

I thought maybe I could get some modelling work, so I contacted a photographer we had met called David Drew Zingg and asked him to take some test shots. I went for the shots with my hair in curlers, because the humidity was such that my hair would frizz in seconds if I didn't keep it under control until I was inside an air-conditioned building. He took some fabulous photos, which resulted in me getting work on whisky and cigarette campaigns. The money I earned was good, and after my failure as a tour guide, it cheered me up.

One evening, there was a loud knock on the front door. The debt collector for the credit card company we owed money to had found us. Michael went through his pockets and my handbag, took all the cruzeiros he found and offered them to the guy to report back to the company that we were nowhere to be found. No doubt the debt collector was becoming a rich man.

After this incident, we decided we had better leave the apartment, and much to my delight, we moved to Ipanema, where there was always music and dancing and a constant air of festivity.

To help pay the rent, we took in a lodger, Joel, an American who taught English to adult students. He liked cocaine, the stay-awake drug, and so there was always a supply – which, I hasten to say, I rarely used, although I had a taste then that in later years did me no good.

Michael was progressing with his movie, a love story called *Intimidade* (*Intimacy*). The two leads were both actors well known in Brazil, which helped him to raise finance after Globo pulled out. Unfortunately his budget was not enough to support a flat in Ipanema, but one of his backers, a wealthy businessman, offered to let us his house in Búzios, a village about a hundred miles along the coast from Rio. He clearly fancied me, and I had a suspicion that the next-to-nothing rent he wanted might involve me having to be very nice to him, but I said nothing. So after only a few weeks in Ipanema, we waved goodbye to Sugarloaf Mountain and lovely Rio and set off on the three-hour drive to our next home.

Búzios turned out to be an idyllic place. There were the most beautiful sandy beaches I had ever seen or imagined, and whereas the sea in Amaralina had been rough, here the greeny-blue water was clear and warm, lapping gently on the golden sand.

Although it is now a thriving beach resort, known as the Saint-Tropez of Brazil, with hotels lining the seafront, in 1974 Búzios was little more than a hamlet. The only signs of life as we arrived were a few fishermen. There was one café bar and no hotels.

Our cottage was small and simple, but it was adequate, apart from a few small gaps where the windows had been put in badly. After depositing me, the children and Edvaldo, Michael returned to Rio to stay with friends. I never asked which friends and he never told me. We had brought food with us, and I went to put it in the fridge, but it didn't work. I tried to switch on the lights, but they didn't work either. Electricity in Búzios, it seemed, was touch and go. Sometimes it was on the blink for several days, but at the start of our stay there, the natural beauty of the place was so breathtaking that it made up for the lack of modern conveniences.

The café bar sold a few necessities, such as milk, bread, and the staple of Brazilian diets, black beans. If I wanted meat or green vegetables, I had to travel by bus to the nearest town, Cabo Frio, an hour and a half's journey away – longer if the bus broke down, which it regularly did.

Most of the men in the village, except for the fishermen, hung out in the bar, while the women did all the work. I was keen to make friends, but I soon came to realize that the villagers viewed me as an oddity. I was the strange Englishwoman who had landed in their midst with two small children, no husband (to speak of) and a young Brazilian servant.

We were happy for the first few months. We explored all the little beaches, and the children learned to swim. Claudia made friends with a family who had children her age and often spent time with them. She told me they didn't use knives and forks; they sat around in a circle eating from a big bowl with their hands. William, now two and a few months, was trying to talk, but his speech was confused, with some words in English and some in Portuguese.

Michael visited us most weekends, bringing a little money for me and presents for the children. Those were happy weekends. Sometimes he brought friends, one of whom gave me two cassette tapes, Pink Floyd's *The Dark Side of the Moon* and Mike Oldfield's *Tubular Bells*. I played them over and over again, when the electricity worked; they were my sole entertainment.

When Michael left at the end of the weekend, we would drive together to Cabo Frio, leaving the children with Edvaldo. After a tearful goodbye, I would do the shopping and catch the bus back.

Very occasionally, the landlord paid a social visit. My initial instinct about him had been right, but since he was charging us the tiniest of rents, which we couldn't pay, to keep a roof over our heads I put up with his ham-fisted attempts to seduce me. The other reason I was nice to him was because I realized that if we were to stay in Brazil, I needed to make a living. I had begun to think of a fashion business, not unlike Biba, which was a hugely successful iconic fashion store selling the most affordable and funky clothes of the sixties and seventies. Looking around the shops in Rio, I had only seen very expensive clothes. There didn't seem to be a fun middle market. For a foreigner to have a business in Brazil, one had to have a Brazilian partner, so he might be a very useful friend.

Edvaldo had not left our side since Amaralina, and he had been a great help to me, but after a few weeks in Búzios he started behaving very strangely. He was spending less and less time keeping an eye on the children and more and more time getting drunk with the men of the village. When he was home with us, he started wanting to wash my feet and kiss me. I was very concerned about his strange and inappropriate behaviour, and I tried talking to him, but he refused to listen, so I had no choice but to let him go. I had no idea then of the consequences this would bring.

One late afternoon, returning from a walk with the children, I found all the windows and doors of our little house wide open. Hundreds of marimbondos, giant wasps, had flown into the house and were clinging to the ceilings inside.

I stood terrified, not knowing what to do. As luck would have it, two young Argentinian men – who it turned out were escaping the military draft in their country – were passing, and I implored them to help us. They found long sticks of wood, which they set fire to, and we went into the house holding the flames up as high as we could. The horrible creatures flew out to escape them, and we were saved. I couldn't thank the young men enough.

I felt certain that it was Edvaldo, furious at being fired, who had allowed the creatures into our house. And this was not the only incident. After he left us, money disappeared from the tin where I kept it, and when I went to the café bar, the men who drank there would hiss at me, and sometimes stones would land near my feet as I approached. Goodness knows what he had told them. It reminded me of the Greek film *Never on Sunday*, in which a call girl played by Melina Mercouri was treated in the same way.

Sula, the eldest daughter of the family Claudia was friends with, came to help me, and I started sending her to the café bar for supplies.

We had been in Búzios for several months and it no longer felt idyllic. I was treated like a pariah by the local people, money was desperately short, and Michael's visits had become sporadic at best. Then the marimbondos got their revenge when one stung my leg. I reacted to the poison so violently that my leg swelled up and I couldn't walk. I began to feel desperate, and wrote in my diary:

The heavy rain of the last 24 hours has turned into a steady drizzle. I sit here freezing cold. I cannot close the windows because I will be left with no light. The electricity in this remote area of Brazil has been cut off for 2 days. I have one warm sweater between the three of us. I cannot walk. My foot is swollen as big as a balloon from various infections after the marimbondo bite and I have a pain in my bladder which I suspect is cystitis as a result of walking barefoot on cold stone floors, but miracle of miracles I found three pairs of enormous woolly socks which with some effort and pain go over my swollen foot. This morning I had to spend half of my fortune on the purchase of water for this uncomfortable, leaky house. It seems incredible . . . a whole 20 cruzeiros on water when there is a bloody great sea on my doorstep, and rain pouring in through every crack in the roof. And what of my husband? What of the man I married? The cocksure, arrogant, irrepressible, unsupportable, lusty go-getter who all the 14-year-old girls used to scream over? God knows where he is or what he's doing.

Last night I cried myself to sleep only to wake up an hour later worrying about the meat going bad because of the electricity cut. So I got up to cook it by candlelight. It was a tiny bit off, but I put enough garlic and vinegar on it not to notice.

The local village idiots have put Macumba curses on me. According to them, I have slept with the fat 60-year-old owner of my house. That is why I am inflicted with a swollen leg and foot, and a cold in my bladder. Talk about small-town persecution.

When I was able to hobble a bit, I would go and sit on the beach as I had done in Malibu. Going through some old papers years later I found the following:

> Can you believe this conversation I just had? I got to the word I and a little boy about six years old walks onto the little beach where I am sitting writing, and says, 'I got six friends, how many have you got?' I tell him, I don't know. I say, what do you mean by friend? but his mind, that wandering bundle of imagination which hasn't yet been totally corrupted to allow him to realize he's not real, has already wandered and he tells me it takes 14 hours to get here. From where? What a lucky, lucky boy! Six friends and only 14 hours to get here. I'll never get here, not in 14 hours, 14 days or 14 years. I wonder what it takes to get here.

I wrote a lot more, none of which says much for my sanity at the time.

I somehow managed to pull myself together. I asked the fishermen if they would like English lessons in return for fish. They didn't want to learn English, but they did want to understand the lyrics of Cat Stevens songs, and others like 'California Dreamin'' – which made me grimace, thinking back to Michael's drug-fuelled friendship with John Phillips.

For a short time we lived on fish and the wild red peppers that grew everywhere. But when William got sick with dehydration, I was beside myself with worry. Claudia wasn't doing well either. I had to get them to civilization soon, not only for their health, but for my own sanity. It was time to go home, but we had a problem. Our visas had run out during the time I had hepatitis, and I had never renewed them, so we needed to get permission to leave.

I sold my little alarm clock to one of the fishermen, which gave me enough money for a return bus fare to Rio. Leaving Claudia with Sula and her family, William and I set off for the city, but after a long and exhausting day being sent from one department to another, we returned to Búzios forlorn and unsuccessful.

The next day, Michael suddenly appeared. I told him we'd had enough; we were leaving Brazil. He seemed relieved, and gave me a little money. William and I returned to Rio to try again, but with the same result. On my third attempt, I took both children with me, with instructions that when I gave the signal, they were to make as much noise and create as much chaos as possible. At the government offices, we were finally admitted to the room of the judge who could stamp our passports. From the moment we entered, his expression told me he was going to refuse, so I gave the children the signal and they started running round the office, shrieking, pulling books and papers from shelves and opening drawers and throwing the contents on the floor. The judge immediately stamped our passports and told us to get out. Well done, Claudia and William.

We left the country a couple of days later. I had no idea where Michael was at this point. All I knew was that he was staying in Brazil. Whether it was to finish his film or continue an affair, I shall never know.

It was August 1975, and we had seen two summers and two winters come and go in Brazil. My children needed an education and I needed to see my parents.

I also needed to do something with my life.

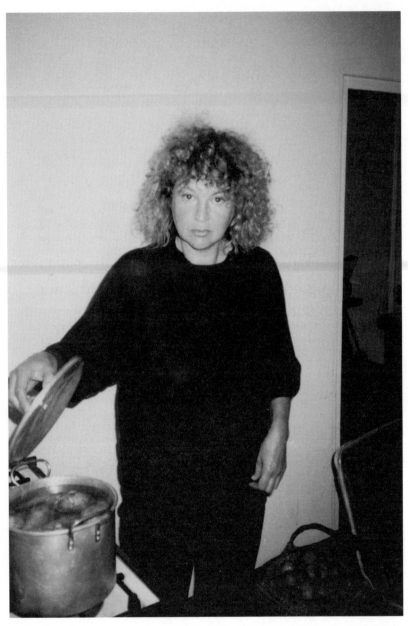

Cooking a cassoulet on return from Brazil and looking rather glum.

Chapter Six

What Now?

———

I returned to England and the safety of my family with my two small children suffering from mild malnutrition and worms. I was completely penniless.

My priority was to restore my children's health and begin their education. Claudia was already nearly a year behind her contemporaries. Next, I needed to find work so I could put food on the table. My parents helped me initially, as did social services, who wrote a strongly worded letter to my husband in Brazil informing him that he and not the taxpayer was responsible for the welfare of his family.

I needed a job, and fast, but Britain was still recovering from the miners' strike and the three-day week, and jobs were scarce. I was ready to do anything. I applied to American Express, who were looking for a secretary. I was interviewed by a large man, too big to fit into his chair, who offered me a job if I gave him a blow job. I didn't. A friend of my parents said that with my languages I was perfect for MI5 and suggested I try there. I looked into it, but the first requirement for those applying to the British Secret Service in 1975 was four British grandparents, and I only had one.

I was near desperation when I bumped into Paul, a man I had met briefly in Brazil. He was walking past me in the street, and we stopped and said hello. I told him I was looking for work, and he said he was importing alpaca jumpers from Peru, and if I could sell them, I had a job. Does one really have choices in life? In my case, if I hadn't encountered this man by chance, it's unlikely I would have found my way into the world of fashion. As it turned out, these brightly coloured alpaca jumpers became the worldwide must-have fashion piece of the mid-1970s and at the same time helped grow my understanding of the fashion business.

I jumped at Paul's offer and started spending long hours on the phone to shops whose details I found in the backs of magazines, making appointments to show them the collection. I sold a lot of jumpers and Paul was pleased with me. He told me about a trade fair in Paris that he thought might be good for sales, so I booked a stand, went on my own and sold thousands more jumpers, mainly to other wholesalers. Within months, I was making Paul a small fortune and at the same time expanding my contact list of buyers and retailers. The problem was that I had to fight him every week to get paid my agreed wage of £50, which just about fed us.

The only excitement and joy I had in my life, other than my children, was a relationship I'd started before going to Brazil, which I now resumed. It had begun one day in Kensington after I had been to visit Michael Chow to see if I could borrow some money. As I got into Michael's red Rolls-Royce convertible to go home, I noticed a man watching me from his Mercedes, parked a short distance away. I drove off and he followed. I stopped in Hyde Park, and he got out of his car and approached me. He was tall, dark and interesting-looking, as well as knowledgeable and witty. So began the most exciting affair, which helped me through some of the darkest moments of my life. He told me he was an underwear salesman – he was not. He was very well known in the advertising world. And he was married. For the next few months, our clandestine weekly meetings took place in various West End hotels. He would leave his room number written on the back of the directory in the phone kiosk in the hotel lobby, which added to the excitement of the wonderful hours we spent together. Neither one of us wanted it to be more than it was, but it added a little spice to both our lives.

After I returned from Brazil, we resumed our affair. I would take a very long lunch break once a week and we would spend it together. Our rendezvous gave me something to look forward to, and a much-needed lift to my spirits. It was exciting, and we enjoyed each other's company immensely.

Michael finally returned from Brazil three months after me and the children. I had no idea who he had been living with there and neither did I care; the deep love between us had somehow evaporated, and reality had set in. Michael had nothing to contribute to our finances and little to our lives. His film career had stalled and his subsequent attempts to get a band together and return to music generally ended up with him getting drunk with the other band members. We didn't row, but the atmosphere between us was strained, and I avoided him as much as possible.

The children and I had settled into a routine. Claudia was now at school, and William was in nursery three days a week. I found a Polish au pair who would help us in return for bed and board. In the afternoons, she would collect the children from school and take them to my mother's before going to her English class. The children adored Mum, and when I picked them up after work, they never wanted to leave her.

One evening in the autumn of 1976, I arrived at my mother's flat to collect the children and she told me she didn't feel well. I advised her to go to bed and rest, and took the children home. At three in the morning, the phone rang. It was the police.

Mum had died and my father was distraught; could I go there immediately? I drove like a lunatic and was there in minutes. Ignoring Dad, I went straight to Mum's bedroom and lay beside her, stroking her hair and talking to her. I am convinced I saw a streak of white light leave her body – her soul or spirit. I stayed with her until the ambulance crew arrived, when they had to tear me away from her.

The cause of her death was never made clear; all we were told was that her lungs had filled with water. Mum was only 55 and she was everything to me: my mother, my best friend and the sister I'd never had. I was utterly bereft. She had been my support throughout my life. Now she was gone, my marriage was no longer a marriage, and my life was a penniless mess.

Her death was a blow for the children too, especially Claudia, who reacted to this great loss by retreating inside herself. She didn't cry and she refused to come with me to the funeral, insisting that she had to go to school. She appeared almost to shut herself off – it was as though she wanted to pretend that it hadn't happened.

Worried about Claudia, devastated by the loss of my mother, I started drinking whisky, which I had always hated. I would also drive for hours, screaming my head off. When this phase passed, my grief turned to rage and anger. Eventually my survival instinct took over. I was ready to fight the world and I was determined to find a way to make a proper living.

Without my mother's help, I needed someone who could work longer hours than an au pair. I couldn't afford a nanny, so I found an agency bringing over homeless young women from various Catholic countries, usually brought up by nuns. It was a complicated and lengthy procedure. In order to obtain a visa for one of these young women, I had to advertise for several months to prove the vacancy could not be filled by a UK citizen. Once proof was submitted to the Home Office, a visa was issued, valid for five years, after which time the person could apply for citizenship. However, this arrangement meant that for the whole of that five years, they could not leave their employment. It didn't occur to me that this was a form of bonded labour and ethically wrong. At the time, I was simply grateful that I had found what I wanted and needed.

Beatrice was an orphan from the Seychelles, brought up by nuns who, she told me, fed the girls bromide so they wouldn't get 'hot'. She was always good-humoured and she kept the children and the house immaculately clean. She was also a stabilizing factor in our lives, since she never went out except to fetch the children from the nearby school when I was busy, or to go to church on Sundays. We were lucky to have her, and

I was grateful for all she did. When her compulsory five years was over, she left us as agreed, and married a man she had met in church.

Alpaca sales were rapidly slowing down. However, at the trade fairs in Paris I had studied other fashion brands and made a note of two labels I really liked that were doing exceptionally well. One was a Scandinavian brand called In Wear, and the other was fashion sportswear called Cacahoute. Neither had representation in the UK. I told Paul, who went to see In Wear and took on the brand for the UK. I asked him for commission on sales and he refused, so I resigned and left him and his jumpers. I later heard on the grapevine that he had imported cocaine in the alpaca jumpers and ended up in prison, but maybe this was just a rumour.

I decided that the only way forward was to take control of my life and have my own business. I was no longer prepared to work for someone else. I had no idea how I was going to achieve this, but I had been good at selling the alpaca jumpers, and the idea of doing something in the fashion world had been forming in my mind for some time. I had even thought about it briefly in Brazil, although it had never been more than a distant notion.

A very charming, sociable, rather portly accountant – let's call him Harry – who was head of a successful commercial fashion company, had started making advances towards me at one of the Paris trade fairs. Prior to my mother's death, I had not responded, but now I did.

I was still seeing the advertising man, who had been kind and sympathetic about my mother's death, but he was only available once a week and Harry was around a lot more, which was what I needed. So I said goodbye to the weekly hotel trysts and started having fun with Harry. He knew a great deal about running a fashion business. I asked him a lot of questions and learned about things like production and pricing. He also took me to the New York trade fair and introduced me to all kinds of people.

Harry liked to drink and to take cocaine. I had tried drugs very occasionally in the past, but now I began taking cocaine with him, and it helped to numb my grief over my mother. There was an amusing incident on the way to New York when security at Heathrow asked him to empty his pockets. He produced an item that looked like a small egg timer, except that it was filled with cocaine. When asked what it was, he replied that it was for his asthma. The security officer returned it to him saying, 'Very good, sir.'

During this period, I was supporting my family by selling two brands I had found and liked. One was Laise Adzer, a handmade, hand-dyed, slightly hippy label made in Morocco, and the other was the Tropical Belt Trading Company, which made sharkskin items for men. Sales were limited, however, and my thoughts turned to the sportswear label that I'd seen in Paris. Talking to one of the other mothers at the school gates, I discovered that she had studied at the Royal College of Art. Susan knew how to cut patterns and understood production. I told her I was thinking of making fashion sportswear and asked if she wanted to give it a go as partners, since I couldn't afford to pay her. She told me she was bored and would love to.

I went to see an old family friend who had said he would help me if I wanted to start a business. He lent me a thousand pounds. With this money I went to the NatWest bank, told them my plans and asked if they would match my thousand with another thousand. After looking me up and down, the manager said, 'You're a woman. What do you know about business?' I refrained from spitting in his eye and went over the road to Barclays, where they agreed to lend me the money I needed to get going.

Michael, who was moping around the house, contributed by helping us with a name. The term Ms for women had just come into use, and he suggested Miz. It seemed right, so Miz it was.

I was ready. My first stop was Leicester, where I found cotton fleece and ribbing. Then I drew dreadful sketches, which my partner, Susan, interpreted with my help. As the pieces were very simple, this worked. We started with six styles: two tracksuit bottoms and four tops. Susan knew of a small factory in Bedford happy to make our designs. The transfer of

Me modelling a Miz top, 1978.

Miz sportswear promotion photo, 1979.

goods was easy, using the Red Star parcel service. What a great system – the factory would drop the parcels at Bedford station, and I collected them at Paddington.

Fashion sportswear hardly existed in 1978 in the UK, and we soon discovered that not only did the retailers want to buy it, so did their customers. The first shops to buy were Joanna's Tent in the King's Road, and Family in Kensington High Street. Sales increased so fast that my living room became more like a warehouse. Boxes that had fitted under the grand piano now spilled out, making it difficult to cross from one side of the room to the other.

My father was prepared to guarantee my overdraft at the bank, so I went to look for premises. In Chepstow Road, off Westbourne Grove, I found the perfect solution: a small retail showroom with glass frontage and a studio at the back just large enough for a cutting table and sewing machine. Downstairs was a basement that could hold our stock. It was a five-minute drive from home for me. But while I felt excited about building my own little business, the situation at home was fast deteriorating.

Michael's father had died, and he was inconsolable. In addition, the lease on our house was coming to an end and the landlord wanted us out and was refusing to negotiate. On top of all this, Harry, my portly accountant, wouldn't let me go, despite the fact that I didn't want to continue our affair. One night as I left work, he was waiting for me in his car. I could see Michael in the distance and, not wanting a confrontation, I jumped into the car and arranged myself low down on the passenger seat, hoping he hadn't seen me. When I returned home a little later, after begging Harry to leave me alone, Michael called me into the bedroom we still shared and hit me across the face, breaking my nose. Just then, my daughter walked in to see blood everywhere. Michael later explained that he had seen me get into Harry's car and crouch down, and had assumed I was going down on him. If he had stopped to think, he would have known it was highly unlikely, since I intensely disliked performing this act.

This event was the final straw for me, the absolute end of our marriage. I had put up with economic stress, infidelity and madness, but I was not going to put up with physical abuse. I asked our lodger to leave and moved into his bedroom. Michael subsequently became increasingly abusive, throwing hot tea at me and cutting the wires for the phone. He had never previously been violent – it wasn't like him at all – but his father's death had affected him deeply, his career was in tatters and now his marriage was ending. Increasingly alarmed by his behaviour, I consulted a lawyer, who helped me to get a court injunction to prevent Michael from coming near me.

Furious, he went to live in his father's flat in Notting Hill Gate.

Several months later, when he had calmed down and become himself again, he sued me for custody of the children. I was horrified. In the build-up to the court case, I went through many sleepless nights, agonizing over what to do. I knew it would get very ugly if we went to court. Michael had already made it clear that he was going to claim I was an alcoholic – although I wasn't at that stage – and to counter him, I would have brought up his drug use. I couldn't bear the thought of seeing our children, then just eight and ten, dragged through the family court and questioned by lawyers, knowing it would cause them untold hurt and damage. There was also the possibility that the court would find us both unfit parents and take the children away.

On the day we were due in court, I arrived with the children – I had been instructed to bring them so that they could be cross-examined. Michael arrived at the same time, and as we waited to be called, I went over to him and asked to talk. I told him we couldn't do this to the children. He agreed and said he would call off the case if I voided the injunction, let William go and live with him and allowed him to see Claudia whenever he wished.

It made my heart ache to agree, but I felt I had no choice. My only solace lay in knowing that Michael would be a good father to William – whatever else he was guilty of, he adored his children. We told our lawyers that we had reached agreement, and Michael took William to live with him in the flat. I kept William's room ready for him, and in the end, he stayed with me and Claudia a good deal of the time, until eventually, as a teenager, he came to live with us.

Fuelled by anger at life and deep sadness over my failed marriage, my focus – apart from my children – was work, work and more work. It was my salvation and my joy. I loved what we were doing, I was excited by it, and through it I found a degree of self-belief, despite all the headaches that were inevitably a part of building a business. I was driven by a relentless determination that at times amazed me.

A few months after we moved into the Chepstow Road showroom, there was a huge setback. Susan told me she and her husband were going to breed chickens in the country, and she left taking all her designs with her. I knew her husband's family had a small factory in the East End producing inexpensive clothing, but I didn't think anything of it, and in any case, there was nothing I could do about it. Subsequently she and her husband built up a relatively successful business selling our sportswear designs to health clubs, gyms and sports clubs.

I was angry, but by this time my attention had turned to fashion rather than sportswear, and I approached Tessa, another Royal College of Art graduate I had met through Susan. She told me that her greatest skill was pattern cutting, especially trousers. She had generous thighs and had cut a trouser pattern that made them look perfectly slim. Tessa remains to this day the very best trouser pattern cutter I have ever worked with.

Not having learned my lesson, I asked her to join me as a partner. She was delighted, and we went to work. Given her talent, I decided we would concentrate on trousers before expanding our range. Through the grapevine I had heard of a warehouse in Sentier, the Paris garment district, where French couture houses and top brands sent their seconds, mistakes and surplus fabrics. I went to Paris and bought all the meterage they had of a fine stretch corduroy, and we made a type of ski trouser with a band under the foot. Miss Selfridge ordered as many as we could make.

Unfortunately, the warehouse in Paris never had more than a few hundred metres of any fabric, so after the trousers, we made whatever we could out of the fabrics I bought. On my next visit I found a plain medium-weight wool out of which we made scarf coats. They sold so well that French Connection copied them. I sued them and won.

Very slowly we began expanding our range, adding jackets and trousers to go with the scarf coat. Next came a couple of dresses and a few tops. At this point we were selling one-offs. I would buy a fabric in Paris, we would make a style and sell it, and with the money I would return to Paris to buy another fabric, and so on. I was learning all the time, and my awareness of how much money and time it would cost to make proper collections twice a year was growing. The bank's confidence in me was also growing. I had left the Bedford factory and found another one only a 40-minute drive from our studio. They were happy to make whatever quantity we could sell, and would also quality-control the pieces so there was one less thing for us to do in our small basement.

We were making enough money to employ a full-time machinist to make first samples, and a driver to collect and deliver orders between Miz, the factory and the shops. Finally we brought in a very inexperienced young designer straight out of college. The brief I gave her was to design wearable, comfortable fashion, but with an edge. I was still developing my ideas and looking for those areas where there was an available niche market. A few retailers from Europe and around the UK began to hear of us and started ordering from the showroom. The government's ECGD (Export Credits Guarantee Department, later to become UK Export Finance) was a huge help. They insured all exports and gave us a percentage of the invoice on shipping.

Miz was slowly but surely growing, but problems were looming. My partner, Tessa, had decided to fall in love with an American on the make. I told her I had stood behind him at the bank when he was unable to withdraw £5, but she wouldn't listen; she was mad about him and totally under his influence. It was obvious to me that he wanted to take over our little business and I was the obstacle in his way, but Tessa was blind. He began to make my life hell. He would lock me out of the office, lie to customers about my involvement in the business, refuse to pass on phone messages and leave empty bottles, beer cans and other rubbish on my desk.

The situation became intolerable. I called my solicitor to explain what was going on, and I also called my father, who was guaranteeing our bank loan. We arranged a meeting with Tessa and the boyfriend, at which my elderly dad had to stand while the American sat with his feet up on the only desk in the room. I wanted to put him on the cutting table and snip him up into small pieces, but instead I offered Tessa £5,000 to get out. After a discussion with her lover, she turned down the offer and reversed it, offering me the same amount to leave. The stock and studio equipment were worth a great deal more than £5,000, but I couldn't work with the pair of them, and I couldn't raise any more than that to get them out, so I took their offer, knowing that in their hands my first company would rapidly go bankrupt. It did, and I later heard that the boyfriend had been deported.

Finally, after five years of Miz, I had learned my lesson. No more partners. It was time to go it alone.

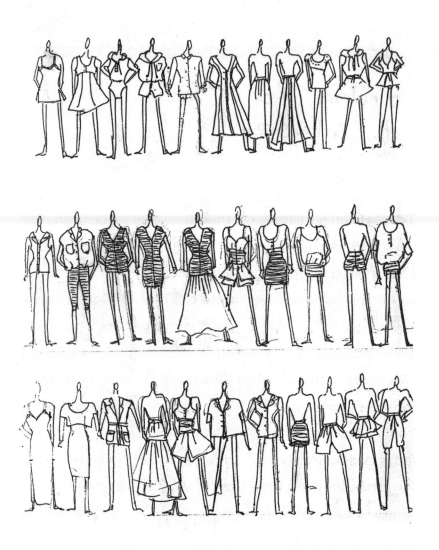

Matchstick sketches sent by Andrea Sargeant for the
summer 1986 collection.

Chapter Seven
The Birth of Ghost

———

The night after I left Miz to the tender care of Tessa and her boyfriend, my mind was in a whirl. I was in shock. I knew I had to start again immediately, while the momentum was still there, but how? I went out to dinner with Katharine Hamnett, a friend and brilliant designer whose clothes I had always admired. We drank lots of wine and joked about doing a collection together called Ghost. We would have a robot taking the orders and no one would know who was behind the label. I decided to run with it. The name really appealed to me. My father had been a ghostwriter for several African presidents; I would be the ghost behind my new fashion business.

It was early 1983, I had been involved with the fashion business, in one way or another, for seven years, and I had become increasingly aware of the lack of good, well-priced, functional feminine fashion for all ages and body types.

Women had to multitask, so their clothes needed to be practical, whether running for a bus, doing the school run, washing up or going to a meeting. Comfort, I reasoned, was also vital, since comfort equals confidence. Women's bodies expand or contract depending on the time of the month, or after a big dinner, so it was important the fabrics had a degree of natural stretch. Who has confidence when trying to pull down a skirt or sit in a certain way so as not to show a bulge somewhere? In order to compete with men, women were dressing in uncomfortable structured suits. What I wanted was the opposite of power dressing; clothes that expressed women's femininity, but which could also be thrown into the washing machine and tumble dried, and which didn't need ironing. I had a horror of ironing ever since I had been expected to iron Michael's shirts.

I registered my new company and then began my search for a designer who would understand my concept. I started by phoning fashion public relations consultant Lynne Franks. I had met her through Harry, and we had become friends. Lynne had started out in 1969, aged 21, working from her kitchen table, her first client being our mutual friend Katharine Hamnett with her first fashion label, Tuttabankem. By the time I met her, she was rapidly becoming the best and foremost PR in the country, with a string of fashion labels among her clients. She laughed when I told her the name of my new company, and joked that it didn't stand the ghost of a chance. She invited me to come to her showroom, where she was showing collections by graduates who had recently left Saint Martin's School of Art. There I found Andrea Sargeant. I loved her collection and got in touch to explain my concept. She understood it and agreed to collaborate with me. The hitch was that she was working for an Italian fashion house and was keen to stay in Italy. I wasn't sure this would work, but since she was the designer I wanted, I agreed.

My next step was to raise some money and set up a studio, since Tessa had commandeered Chepstow Road. After long negotiations with the landlord of our house with the lift, I had agreed to move out for £75,000. The bank had agreed to lend me a further £45,000, and with the £120,000 I planned to buy a very nice house on Ladbroke Road, where we could live and I could also set up my business. Then Michael was sued for bankruptcy, and since we were still married, I had to pay his debts. I was left with £13,000, not enough to buy anything, and the children and I were out on the street.

My father came to my rescue. He had bought a crumbling house in Kensal Road, a run-down part of North Kensington, for £17,000, with the intention of using it as offices. It was such a dangerous area that even taxi drivers wouldn't venture there; they called it the Wild West. He had never used the house, so he said we could live there. With the £13,000 I had left, I put in a bathroom and kitchen, and the children and I moved in with our dog Woofy. He had been given to the au pair who took over after Beatrice had left a couple of years earlier, and when that au pair left too, we kept the dog. His mother was a Portobello Road German Shepherd and his father an aristocratic Airedale Terrier from Knightsbridge. He had often come to work with me at Miz, and on one occasion had leapt to my defence, flying through the air to attack a drunk who had wandered into the showroom and threatened me.

Woofy was a very intelligent and independent dog. He frequently went out for walks on his own, and generally made his own way home safely, barking at the door to let us know that he was back. I did have to rescue him occasionally, though; he once followed a bitch on heat to Whitechapel, and he loved visiting Battersea Dogs Home. He would jump on any van he thought might be going there, knowing I would fetch him when the staff discovered him and phoned me.

The man who had given our au pair the puppy was a good-looking Jamaican Rastafarian and would-be soul singer. He had become a friend of mine, and as he was well known in Kensal Town, he told all the local gangs and troublemakers to look after us, which meant I was safe to walk Woofy at any time of the day or night.

My one-eyed dog, Woofy, 1986.

I was buzzing. I had a home, even if it wasn't exactly the Ritz. There were no bailiffs at the front door, no court summonses, no moaning out-of-work husband and no demanding lover either. Claudia and I lived upstairs, where there was also a bedroom for William when he came, and I made a studio in our big front room, which led through to the office and kitchen.

When I split from Miz, I had told the factory to send the current order to me. That gave me a little stock, which I stored in the garage. As for my staff, Christine, the machinist I'd employed at Miz, joined me, as did Jimmy, Miz's driver. And Ali, who had come to us as an au pair, confessed that she longed to be a pattern cutter, so I sent her on a training course, and once she completed it, she came back to work for us too.

I decided there would be no more one-off styles. I had to move forward, get serious and start making proper collections twice a year. My first collection was for winter, so I chose as my starting point machine-washable lambswool, which came in shades of muted blue and green and was warm, comfortable and flattering, since it moulded to the body and had natural stretch. Andrea sent me matchstick sketches, which I interpreted with Ali, before Christine got to work making up the first samples. These were sent to the factory in Hayes in west London that I had switched to during my time with Miz. Once the garments came back, we tie-dyed some of them to create softer layers of shade.

There were some wonderful pieces in this first very small collection. Andrea had designed voluminous lambswool dresses that sold really well, and a close second was her wraparound quilted skirt.

However, at this early stage Ghost was still finding its feet, and it was only with the help of a few loyal customers that we were able to continue. One of these was a German company called Zoom, owned by an extraordinary and wonderful man called Jacques Buisson. Jacques gave Ghost its first big order, for £10,000, which was a huge boost. He also introduced me to a friend and colleague of his called Kurt, a devastatingly attractive man with a grey streak in his hair, who had previously owned a jeans company that several incarnations later became a global brand.

Kurt was charming and thoughtful, and I couldn't help myself; I fell for him in a big way. He was on his second marriage, but he said it was over, and if I'm honest, I was too infatuated to care. He began to travel from Germany regularly to visit me. My father and grandmother adored him, since he spoke French. My father's mother refused to learn English, so they all spoke together in French and shared war stories. Both of Kurt's parents had lost their families in Auschwitz.

I also used to visit him in Düsseldorf, where Jacques Buisson would lend us his beautiful apartment. Sadly, Jacques became ill, and a year later he died of AIDS. He was an early victim; AIDS was just starting to make an impact, and none of us really understood what was happening, but we grieved for a truly wonderful man.

After that first winter collection in 1984, I found myself struggling with cash flow. I had a family to support and staff to pay, plus the cost of Andrea's flights from Italy. The orders we had delivered made just enough money, on paper, to see us through until the spring/summer collection, but only half of what we had delivered had been paid for. Some retailers expected to pay two months after delivery, and this would occasionally stretch until just before they got their next order. I remember one small retailer in Carnaby Street who was being really difficult. I went to talk to them about it, and finding no one in the small office above the shop, I helped myself to all the office paraphernalia I needed and left. I am not proud of this, it wasn't right, but nor was refusing to pay me, and I was fighting to survive and grow a business.

Then I heard about a new venture opening in Kensington High Street called Hyper Hyper. Based on the ground floor of a very large building, this was a kind of indoor market, in which designers could rent a space to sell their designs. It was on the opposite side of the street to Kensington Market, a fabulous eclectic showplace for individual new young designers, as well as a source of wonderful vintage clothes. When Hyper Hyper opened, I immediately rented a stand, which I stocked with everything left over from Miz and the remainder of our winter collection. I hired someone to run the stall and we gave Claudia her first Saturday job there. The sales made all the difference to our cash flow, and I was able to stop chasing late payers and concentrate on our first summer collection.

I racked my brains trying to think of a summer fabric with the qualities of the lambswool we had used, but I still hadn't found the answer when Andrea arrived for a visit looking as if she had put on a whole lot of weight. She took off her coat, and underneath it, wrapped around her, was a yellowish fabric. It had a hard, almost hessian feel, but she explained that when boiled, it became a soft crêpe with a slight orange-peel effect and natural stretch. Not quite believing her, I cut a small piece and put it in a saucepan with boiling water. After it had dried, not only had it changed colour and become almost white, but it was also beautifully soft, slightly crinkled, and stretchy.

Andrea explained that the company she was working for had tried to use it, but the fabric had damaged too easily, which in their opinion meant it was not commercially viable. She had thought it was just what we were looking for, and since she didn't want to be seen walking out with it, she'd found a clever way of bringing it with her.

The name of the supplier was on a little tag. I phoned them immediately and ordered a roll. Excited by the possibilities, I managed to get a last-minute stand at the upcoming fashion trade fair in Olympia. This was our chance to be seen by a wider audience.

The fabric arrived and, working day and night, we managed to make about 12 pieces by the evening before the fair. They included a pair of straight-leg trousers and a floaty A-line skirt, both of which would become Ghost classics, plus a shirt that opened down the back and a wraparound robe. We threw them into the washing machine, then the tumble dryer, and held our breath. When we took them out, I couldn't believe my eyes. The pieces were stunning, a gorgeous off-white, as soft as down, with slight texture and stretch. There was only one problem. Everything had shrunk by at least a third. There was no way we could show these clothes on a tall, skinny model.

I rushed upstairs to Claudia and asked her if she and a couple of her friends would like to earn some pocket money that week while they were on school holidays. She wasn't overjoyed, since she had other plans, but she phoned two friends who loved the idea of modelling, which was how, for the next few days, I showed Ghost's first summer collection on three 14-year-olds.

Whether it was the teenage girls dancing around on our stand or the collection itself, I'm not sure, but an American retailer from Detroit who introduced himself as Mark climbed onto our stand and shouted, 'It's money in the bank, folks!' And that was that, we were swamped. For our first winter collection we had taken orders for £25,000, including the £10,000 from Jacques, but for this, our second collection, the orders came to £250,000. Overnight our order book had increased by 900 per cent.

I was stunned and thrilled, but how on earth was I going to produce the garments? I didn't have the money, the company infrastructure or a good enough understanding of shrinkage and dyeing. Did I go to the bank first, or the fabric supplier? How much fabric would I need? What if I couldn't get enough?

I decided there was no point going to the bank if I couldn't get the raw material, so I phoned the fabric supplier in Italy and told them we would need a minimum of 10,000 metres. To my horror, they replied that there was a problem. The only yarn that could be used to make the fabric we had sampled came from a company in Germany called Enka, and supplies were limited. It was derived from wood specially grown for this purpose and was fully biodegradable, hence the limited supply. What they had was reserved for a few upmarket international brands.

I pleaded. I told the Italians to tell Enka they would now have a UK company who would advertise Enka viscose on all their garments. What Enka produced was the Rolls-Royce of viscose yarn and had nothing to do with the cheap shiny rayon I remembered from my youth, which had been in heavy use after the Second World War. Enka viscose was the equivalent of using cashmere rather than plain wool.

After much pleading and many conversations, Enka and the Italian company agreed to supply me with just enough fabric to cover my orders, but not enough to make any stock. With problem number one solved, I went to the bank with my orders and asked for finance. The response was lukewarm, but agreement was reached on condition I found a guarantor. My father was always generous, but on this occasion he was nervous. I convinced him by telling him that Mum would have left me half the flat if she had made a will, so it was only right that he should now guarantee my business loan. Eventually he agreed.

I needed someone to help me with the money and invoicing side of the business. Then I remembered that one of my few loyal customers had a young brother who was an accountant. I got his phone number and asked him if he would like to join me, and he said yes. His name was Martin Hudson, and from the start he was an invaluable help in organizing, growing and sustaining the business and keeping me calm. He was always cheerful and unflappable, no matter what was happening. With his help we set up a simple computer system that enabled us to enter our orders and estimate fabric quantities. Later, as we grew, I wanted to develop our own system, but under pressure from my accountants and solicitor, I was told I had to buy a 'proper' system from a computer company who knew what they were doing. The company I went to held me over a barrel every year, telling me that if I didn't upgrade, at huge cost, they wouldn't be able to fix any problems. I never forgave myself for listening to the so-called professionals instead of developing the system I wanted and needed.

I now had the fabric I needed, but not the facility to boil or dye it. I needed somewhere capable of washing thousands of garments at 90 degrees and then dyeing them, since I couldn't just sell white, especially as the colour we achieved after boiling wasn't a pure white.

After some research, I settled on a company near Leicester. It had been set up by the Stevenson family in the late 19th century and had once employed two thousand people. In 1984, with the decline of the British textile industry, the workforce numbered less than five hundred. To my delight, they were more than happy to take on our work.

Finally I had to sort out potentially the trickiest problem of all – how to deal with shrinkage. I started by buying a washing machine that would wash at 90 degrees. We reasoned that if we took a square metre of fabric, washed it at 90 degrees and tumble dried it, we could then measure the warp and the weft and add the percentage by which it had shrunk to our patterns. The reasoning was perfect, but the reality wasn't, and many of the pieces weren't an exact size, but since the fit was determined largely by the wearer's body shape, it didn't matter too much. That being said, all my effort went into making every piece flattering.

Having laid the foundations for production, we started on our first big orders. Patterns were cut but they had not yet been computerized, and because of the shrinkage added on, we had huge pieces of card everywhere, which took up a lot of space. First samples were made and sometimes remade several times before sending them to the factory, after which they had to go to Stevenson's to be shrink-washed. The production process was laborious and slow, and the Hayes factory let us keep the finished garments at their premises since space in Kensal Road was limited.

Life was quite mad, and there was little separation between work and home; it all merged into one. After a late night working with a bottle of wine, I would drag myself out of bed early to make breakfast for Claudia, and William if he was with us, and then drive them to school, desperately trying to get them there on time. Thankfully, their schools were near to each other and not too far away from home. William was at Upper Latymer and Claudia at Godolphin and Latymer, the same school that had tried to educate me. They had become independent schools, but thanks to Margaret Thatcher, they now offered a number of assisted school places for those without means to pay. Both my children had these, and I was hugely grateful; it meant that all I had to pay for were their uniforms and lunches. I knew the head, since she'd been my history teacher when I was there and, remembering kneeling in the draughty assembly hall in a skirt, I asked her if I could design a pair of simple grey trousers to add to the uniform. Her reply? 'I see you are still heretical.' I took that as a no.

After the school rush and the arrival of my staff, I usually retired to my bedroom above the makeshift studio to get properly dressed, put my make-up on and plan the day.

No matter how busy things were, I always found time to make lunch for everyone. It wasn't merely altruistic; there was nowhere near Kensal Road in those days where they could get something decent to eat, and I needed my staff well fed and healthy. Plus it worked better for the business if we all took a break at the same time, since everyone's work was connected. The bonus was that if I cooked a huge meal, there was food left over ready for my children when they got home from school. I shopped at weekends in Portobello Market, where I knew all the street vendors, and then made huge casseroles and salads.

Suddenly it was February 1985, and the shops that had ordered from us wanted to know when they would get their spring/summer orders. The finished garments arrived from Stevenson's, and I opened the boxes excitedly and started hanging them up, then stared in complete disbelief. Horror of horrors, some of the garments had holes in them and on many the seams were frayed and falling apart. I wept. I had so much riding on this and had thought this fabric such a brilliant idea. We had factored in the shrinkage, so what had gone wrong?

When I had finished howling, I phoned the supplier and accused him of selling us faulty fabric. He explained to me that viscose has no wet strength. If one were to put the edge of a coin on wet viscose, it would make a hole. If Stevenson's had used a hard-edged steel-type implement to take the garments out of the washing machine rather than a wooden one – or best of all, taking them out by hand – this would account for the holes. He suggested the frayed seams were caused by not including enough seam allowance.

He was right, I realized it as soon as he said it. We had added a third extra to the main pattern, but not on the seams.

I thought of the Italians who had given up on this fabric and sympathized.

Was I going to give up too? No, I most certainly wasn't. I went straight down to Portobello Market and, by asking around the second-hand clothing stalls, found two young women who could sew and who agreed to help me. For the next few nights, the three of us stayed up sitting on my staircase – situated between the studio where the clothes were and the kitchen where the coffee was – sewing up all the seam slippages by hand.

By the end, we were cross-eyed with exhaustion, our fingers cramped and sore, but the seams were intact and the orders went out, albeit a little short because we couldn't do anything about the ones with holes in them.

Miraculously, Ghost sold brilliantly everywhere, and we didn't have a single complaint. I was thrilled. We were on our way.

Me in Ghost's first warehouse, 1988.

Photograph taken by Andrew Macpherson.

Chapter Eight

Up and Running

———

Ghost took its first baby steps on the runway in September 1985 when the owner of Hyper Hyper invited us, along with seven other new, young designers, to take part in London Fashion Week, with a show in the Pillar Hall in Olympia. Each of us was allotted three minutes.

The show was called Hy-Lites, and for our segment we had 'Andrea Sargeant for Ghost' lit up behind the runway. We were showing clothes for the following spring and summer, and I remember they looked like white clouds. As the models danced, the skirts, dresses and tops, all loose and with slits in them, seemed to dance too. Two male models wore robes that could have been dressing gowns or beach throw-overs, with yellow ribbons tied around them, showing that Ghost clothes could be worn by anyone – we were making gender-neutral clothes well before it became fashionable.

It was exciting to see our work come to life in this way, and the applause as our models paraded up and down was wildly enthusiastic, so I hoped for a good response. Following the show, a notable fashion journalist, Iain R. Webb, gave us an excellent review, but even so I was stunned when our orders over the next few weeks doubled again to £500,000. It seemed that word had spread among retailers that our clothes were flying off the rails.

Half a million pounds seemed impossibly huge, and an order book that big presented a dilemma; I didn't think we could handle this volume of orders from the ground floor of our little house in Kensal Road, but I didn't yet feel confident enough to look for proper commercial premises. I didn't want to move us to a more suitable workplace until I knew we would continue growing and this wasn't just a dream. So we stayed where we were, used every inch of space we had and worked day and night to fill the orders.

After the success of the first show, Hyper Hyper's owner planned another for March 1986, to be called Hi-Priestess. Realizing that Ghost was their biggest asset, they gave us more time on the runway, and more control over models and music.

We were showing the winter collection for 1986, and our Italian fabric supplier had decided I was serious and had sent us lots of samples, all with the same quality of viscose yarn but woven in different weights. There was a featherlight georgette, as well as a heavier version, a padded satin and a quilted fabric, some of them ideal for the winter collection. We hadn't yet tried colour, but we did produce some pieces in black as well as white, and we experimented with styles and shapes, always keeping comfort, ease of movement and femininity as our guiding principles.

For this second Hyper Hyper show, I could choose my own models, and I asked Claudia and her friends. Claudia was 16 and she made a great model – she was a similar height to me, almost five foot eight, and she was gorgeous, with a cloud of curly dark hair. I couldn't afford to pay models; besides which, she and her friends not only loved being part of the experience, they brought wonderful energy and enthusiasm to it. Claudia also put together the music for the show. I had known that her talent and knowledge of music would create a wonderful atmosphere, and it did.

One of our early models was Claudia's friend Rachel Weisz, who would go on to be a hugely successful actress. She was just two months younger than Claudia and they were very close. The two of them danced down the runway to the disco hit 'Shame, Shame, Shame' by Shirley & Company, wearing flowing skirts, black knee-length socks and black shoes. Another friend of Claudia's who would later become a big success and who also appeared in this show was Neneh Cherry, a singer and songwriter whose stepfather was the legendary jazz trumpeter Don Cherry. Neneh was in a band called the Slits, and boy, could she dance. She danced her socks off.

In the weeks that followed this second show, our orders shot up again, and I knew I had no option but to find Ghost a new home; we had outgrown the house in Kensal Road.

A stone's throw away, on the other side of the road, next to a pub, was an old chapel, once the headquarters for the Notting Hill Carnival. It was for sale, and I went to have a look. Upstairs there were three snooker tables, while downstairs housed a company making cheap foldaway chairs. What a waste of a fabulous space – the dimensions were perfect, as was the natural light.

It was on the market for £163,000, which was a bargain, given the size of it. Luckily, I had developed a friendly relationship with Ian, our bank manager at Barclays. Knowing my love of tennis, he had taken me to the men's final at Wimbledon the previous summer, when 17-year-old sensation Boris Becker had won.

I went to see Ian and told him that our orders had doubled and I needed a loan to buy a commercial building to house Ghost's growing business. He agreed, the loan was secured on the house in Kensal Road, and in the autumn of 1986, I bought what became known as the Chapel. It seemed a fitting abode for Ghost.

Before we moved in, we held a huge christening party. By this time I had got to know a lot of people in the fashion business, in part through my membership of the Fashion Industry Action Group (FIAG), which would later become the British Fashion Council. I had been elected to join back in 1981, when I was running Miz. At that time Paris was the fashion capital of the world, supported and funded by the French government. Italy was next, with a textile industry second to none, and Germany was investing heavily in new machinery for production. And England? We trailed behind with an ever-dwindling textile industry, six uncoordinated fashion shows a year and a handful of trade shows.

FIAG had been set up to promote and coordinate British fashion, but I soon became extremely impatient with it. I was argumentative and had far too many ideas for the men in suits, who more than outnumbered the women, and after three years I'd had enough and left.

Young designers Jasper Conran and John Galliano, then in their mid-twenties and just starting out on their careers, both occasionally attended FIAG meetings, so I had got to know them and they came to our christening party along with Ossie Clark, whose heyday in the sixties and seventies saw him design for everyone from Mick Jagger to Liza Minnelli. Ossie had become a close friend of mine; his son Albert was at Upper Latymer School with William, and a few years later they would go on to open a restaurant together.

Our christening party was overflowing with designers, musicians, models and photographers, many of whom I didn't know. Word had got round. I was especially happy because Kurt came over from Germany, and that night he told me that he and his wife were getting divorced and soon he would be coming to live with me and help me with the business.

The evening was a wonderful, chaotic riot, and everyone misbehaved, so much so that I had to get an expensive firm of cleaners in post-party to make the place usable again. But once the cleaning was finished and all the walls had a new coat of white paint, we moved in. I put in a large kitchen at the back of the ground floor, behind which were the toilets and washing facilities. At the front, at street level, a very large purpose-built cutting table was installed for the pattern cutters. Ali couldn't manage alone at this point, so I hired Teresa, a very experienced pattern cutter who had come from the respected fashion label Frank Usher. Teresa was very grand. She nearly always had a long cigarette holder complete with cigarette dangling from her lips, and was accompanied by her petite assistant, Marilou.

Next to the cutting table were the sewing machines for our

machinist, Christine. A second machinist, Paul, would come in to help when we were under pressure. They needed to be near the pattern cutters in order to ask questions and clarify problems.

Upstairs at the rear of the building, where there was a lovely vaulted ceiling, I set up the showroom, where first samples were kept and fittings done. And in the front, my clever interior designer friend Ted Walters, who would later create the interiors for all our shops, built three very long parallel desktops. One was for production, headed by a lovely calm woman named Aileen, and a second was for finance and administration, overseen by Martin. At that point we had only ten or so members of staff, but the desks were long enough to accommodate assistants and secretaries as we grew.

I sat at the middle desk, from where I could keep an eye on the entire process. I needed to hear and see everything that was going on, and by placing myself so centrally, I could.

There wasn't enough room for a warehouse, so I rented a cheap one a few minutes' walk away. This was where, in years to come, we would hold our famous warehouse sales, until eventually we outgrew it and had to find a larger space.

Finally, when everything was in place, I stood in the middle of the Chapel and felt incredibly proud. We had a home, the design talent, the orders, the fabric supply and the production in place. And we had the finance to make it all happen.

Outside the Chapel – Ghost HQ, 1994.

The Kensal Road house seemed much bigger now that Ghost had moved out, especially as William had just started at boarding school. Latymer hadn't suited him; he kept getting into trouble for things he hadn't done, and it was making him miserable and me cross, so for the two years in which he was doing his GCSEs, we moved him to a lovely school where he was very happy.

Claudia and I were rattling around, but not for long, as it turned out – she announced that she wanted her boyfriend to move in with us. She was 16 and he was at least 5 years older than her, and I didn't particularly like him, so I was horrified. However, when she saw the look on my face, she told me that if I didn't let him move in, then she would leave. I was used to being told what to do by my daughter; she had been doing it for years. So against my better judgement, I agreed. At least this way, I thought, she would continue her schooling. This was by no means certain, since the boyfriend was in the music business and the two of them spent a lot of time going to gigs and hanging out with musicians. Claudia was a talented musician herself; she had studied the piano with concert pianist Carola Grindea, in whose house my parents and I had stayed after the war, and she had a beautiful singing voice. I had no objection to her becoming a musician; I just wanted her to take her A levels first.

The lower part of the house, where Ghost had been, was

now empty, so I gave the space to Richard Ostell, a young designer whose work had really impressed me. I encouraged him as much as possible to build his own brand, but his work was architectural, pared down and not obviously commercial. After two years struggling on his own, he joined forces with Ellis Flyte and moved to Camden, where they had some success as Flyte Ostell.

Our move to the Chapel prevented us from having a show in September 1986, but by March 1987, we were ready with our new collection and I felt confident enough to break away from Hyper Hyper to do our own show. By this time I had taken on Lynne Franks to do all our PR. Lynne had a natural flair for publicity, an astonishing book of contacts and enormous energy. She suggested we hold our first show as a tea party at the Groucho, a private club in London's Soho that was fast becoming one of *the* places to be seen. It had opened in 1985, aiming to bridge the gap between stuffy gentlemen's clubs and working men's clubs as a place where both men and women could meet, work, stay and relax. One of the Groucho's founding principles was equality for women – the idea that a woman could sit alone at a bar and not be considered a prostitute was revolutionary back then – and as I knew architect Tchaik Chassay, who was one of the founders, I was given membership as soon as it opened its doors.

All the fashion press and a handful of Lynne's celebrity friends were invited. I was delighted when I spotted the wonderful Jennifer Saunders sipping tea. Jennifer was a good friend of Lynne's and a few years later would write the hugely successful TV sitcom *Absolutely Fabulous*, in which Edina, a chaotic, heavy-drinking, drug-abusing PR, spends her time chasing bizarre fads in an effort to stay hip. Jennifer played Edina and Joanna Lumley played her magazine fashion director friend Patsy, who is even madder and wilder than Edina. Into the mix comes Edina's sensible and long-suffering student daughter Saffy, who tries in vain to curb her mother's excesses.

Rumour had it that Jennifer based Edina on Lynne, and I heard through mutual connections that I was also a source of inspiration. I wasn't sure whether to be flattered or outraged, or even if it was true. Although I do remember that Dawn French came to visit the Ghost showroom one day, and after I had plied her – and myself – with copious amounts of champagne, Claudia appeared and ordered me to stop drinking. It was a scene that could have come straight from *Ab Fab*.

My models for this first solely Ghost presentation included old hands Claudia, Rachel Weisz and Neneh Cherry, along with actress Amanda Donohoe. She had modelled for me back in the Miz days, when she was the girlfriend of pop star Adam

Neneh Cherry at Groucho's Tea Party show, 1987.

Ant. After ending the relationship, she went to drama school, and her first film, *Castaway*, in which she starred opposite Oliver Reed, came out in 1986 to good reviews. There was one male model, a boyfriend of one of the girls, and we also included my Swedish friend Gill's two children, aged eight and ten, for whom we had made smaller versions of a few pieces in the collection.

This was a winter show, and the Italian supplier had made us some wonderful quilted fabric by taking two layers of crepe or satin viscose, placing padding between them and keeping it all in place by embroidering both sides of the fabric. With this we designed coats, jackets, waistcoats and trousers.

Before the show, I was nervous. Waiting backstage, listening to the clink of cutlery and the chatter of our guests, I wondered if Ghost was about to fall flat on its face. I was actually quite shy, and was grateful that I could remain out of sight. Our young models had no such doubts; they danced between the tables with abandon, as the audience sipped their tea and applauded. The show was as memorable for the dancing as for the fashion, but it did demonstrate how wearable the clothes were. At the end, Andrea was there to take a bow, and once it was all over, I was both relieved and happy that it had been a success.

We all worked incredibly hard and the Chapel buzzed with activity as we put in long hours to create clothes that flowed and fitted as I wanted them to. I had a team of people who were excellent at what they did, and I valued them.

One afternoon, Ossie Clark strolled in announcing that he had come to help. I was fond of Ossie; he had been a hugely influential and successful designer, but at this point his life was not going well. He was suffering after the demise of a long relationship, and his fashion partnership with Radley had come to an abrupt end. I'd heard that a Dr Feelgood-type on Harley Street was dispensing substances to him that were not healthy, and it was evident much of the time that he wasn't himself.

Ignoring everything that was going on in our busy workroom, he walked imperiously over to Teresa, looked over her shoulder and then brushed her aside, exclaiming, 'Call yourself a pattern cutter? I'll show you how it's done.' The pattern and fabric on the table were for a bias-cut slip, and Ossie was famous for his bias cut. He turned to our middle-aged machinist, Paul, and said, 'Boy, give me the scissors,' then, ignoring the pattern, began cutting into the fabric, while everyone stood around slightly shell-shocked and bemused. After a few minutes, he finished cutting and left, shouting over his shoulder that he would be round in the evening for vodka and lime.

I broke the frozen silence by announcing that it was lunchtime. I was still providing lunch, even though the numbers had swelled considerably, but by this time I couldn't do it all myself, so I employed a lovely Portuguese woman who cleaned my house and cooked under my guidance.

After lunch, Paul tried and failed to put together the pieces of fabric Ossie had cut. Ossie had been a genius in his heyday, but even he could not cut straight into fabric without a pattern. And at this point his genius days were behind him, although he did make me a beautiful boned dress a few years later for my fiftieth birthday.

While the rest of us dismissed his visit as just Ossie being Ossie, Teresa did not. She felt insulted and outraged by his high-handed attitude, and soon after this she left, trailing Marilou behind her and leaving me with yet another dilemma. We solved it by putting Ali in charge and giving her two interns to train.

Not long after we moved into the Chapel, my divorce from Michael finally came through. I had been trying to divorce him since 1983, when I'd had to use most of my house money to save him from bankruptcy, but he had steadfastly ignored my lawyer's letters and calls until eventually, after three years, the divorce was issued by default.

The day the decree absolute arrived, I realized that more than 17 years after I had married Michael, I was finally free. It felt good.

At around the same time, my wonderful Uncle Dennis died of lung cancer. Still only in his mid-sixties, he had always been a heavy smoker. Now there was no one left on my mother's side of the family, and I felt deeply sad, recalling his visits when I was growing up and the joy he brought to my lonely childhood.

As lovely as he was, he was also very strange, and he had never introduced his wife to any of us. This wife did not invite me or my father to the funeral, which hurt profoundly. Dennis died intestate, and the wife assumed she would inherit everything. However, in part because of her lack of civility, my father insisted I make a claim on his estate, which was worth around £300,000, since he owned a substantial property in Putney. My lawyer contacted her, at which point her lawyers replied that the matter would go to court. It did, some months later, and I was awarded £25,000.

I decided to spend the money on a house by the sea, something I had always wanted. I began searching, but every house I liked was too expensive. Finally, on a visit to Ramsgate in Kent, I spied a tall, thin, tumbledown house built into the cliffs overlooking the sea. It was up for auction and I went along to bid for it. It didn't meet its reserve price, which was more than the £25,000 I had, so it was withdrawn. But shortly afterwards, to my amazement, the owner phoned me and agreed to sell it to me anyway. I was overjoyed.

Bit by bit, with the help of Ted Walters, I brought it back to life. We couldn't do much to the exterior since it was a Grade II listed building, but inside we created a modern kitchen/dining room on the ground floor, a sitting room on the first floor with a very small bedroom off it, a master bedroom on the second floor and an attic room with space for two double mattresses.

We installed the bath in the master bedroom. There wasn't room for one anywhere else and I loved the idea that I could lie in it and look out to sea. I bought a pretty antique desk, which I put by the window, and it was here that I sat and gazed and daydreamed, painting the changing shades of the sea, the sunrise and the sunset. I must have painted more than a thousand colours, and over the years we used them for all Ghost's collections. It makes me happy knowing that Ghost is remembered as much for its beautiful, soft, natural colours as for its flattering fabrics and designs.

Naomi Campbell opening the 1989 show.

Chapter Nine

Heartache

―――

When Kurt arrived, suitcase in hand, to move in with me, I was over the moon. The business was flourishing and now the man I had fallen in love with was by my side.

His presence was gracefully accepted by Claudia and Will, who referred to him cheerfully as 'that mad jeans designer'. On weekday evenings we were sometimes together for supper, but at weekends Kurt and I would disappear to Ramsgate with Woofy. I drove us there in my old silver Citroën, and as there were far fewer cars on the road in those days, the journey took no more than 90 minutes. The sea was a wonderful calming influence for us both after a chaotic week.

Kurt had been involved in the fashion industry for many years, so I asked him to help out with production. He fitted in well with the informal family that was Ghost, and Aileen, who had been handling the ever-growing production demands on her own, welcomed his help in watching over the costings, sorting out problems and making sure the factory wasn't making extra pieces to sell on the side – a practice known as cabbage.

Martin continued to be my rock in finance and administration, Lynne Franks was doing a fabulous PR job, and my staff was growing with astonishing speed. We needed a second person in the warehouse, checking in deliveries and making up orders, and our Portuguese cook and cleaner, Maria, brought in her nephew Carlos to fill the role. Meanwhile Martin took on a secretary, Pippa, and we added a third machinist, Carol – who was also a wonderful musician. Ali had help from several interns, who also helped me. Two of these, Margarita Gosling and Sue Stemp, stayed with Ghost for several years.

My biggest problem was the patterns. Andrea would send her matchstick sketches from Italy, I would decide which of them to make, and Ali would then do her best to interpret them. Ali was not as experienced as Teresa had been, but what she lacked in experience she made up for with enthusiasm and determination. However, you can give the same sketch to two different pattern cutters and get two very different garments, so to get the finished pieces just right and make the style work, I sat in on the fitting of every sample, changing sleeves, moving seam lines or necklines, deciding lengths and adjusting to make the garment more flattering on the body and more interesting as a piece. This was where my real creative skill lay. I had a strong sense of what I wanted and how a garment should look, and I directed the alterations until I was satisfied.

I was running a rapidly growing business, which felt both wonderful and – occasionally – terrifying. I tried to plan, but more often my decisions were the result of inspiration rather than calculation. I don't believe I had a vision of a huge business; I just wanted it to work, to feel secure financially, and to be recognized as a credible fashion brand.

I worked incredibly hard, often arriving at the Chapel early in the morning and staying late into the evening. I had never thought of myself as a driven person, but that was what I had become. Ghost was my baby. Every decision had to be okayed by me and everyone depended on me.

I never got enough sleep, and to keep going, I began fuelling myself with cocaine and alcohol in the evenings. I had crossed paths with cocaine in Brazil but had done little more than sample it. However, Harry had not only reintroduced me to it, he'd made it so constantly available that in retrospect I think it was his way of keeping me at his side, so that I would never wander. Now Kurt and I would have a couple of glasses of red wine and a line of cocaine in the evening, and that gave me the energy to keep going. I was very controlled in the amount I took, viewing it in the same way as putting petrol in a car – as far as I was concerned, I needed fuel to function, and this did the trick. It also made me fearless. I had always been shy, and had never found it easy to give orders or make speeches or deal with the many buyers, suppliers and businesses that I encountered every day, but cocaine gave me self-confidence.

Then one night three months or so after Kurt arrived, my world fell apart. We were just finishing dinner when the doorbell rang. I went to open the door and there was a young woman holding a small girl and a suitcase. She told me she had come to get her husband, who had given her this address. I stared at her. I could feel the colour draining from my face and my mind was in turmoil. Was this the woman Kurt had told me he was divorcing? I called to him and watched in disbelief as the two of them greeted each other warmly before he invited her in.

As his wife sat with a coffee and fed the little girl, I pulled Kurt into the next room. 'What the hell's going on?' I screamed.

He didn't seem in the least bothered. 'Don't worry,' he said. 'We're separated. I'm not leaving you; she just wants to be nearer to me for the sake of our daughter. We need to find her a place to stay.'

I should have thrown him out then. But I was desperately in love with him, so somehow I managed to engage my brain and phone my driver, Jimmy. He owed me a favour as I'd given him work when he was down and out, and I knew he had a large flat not far away, so I explained the problem and asked if the wife and child could stay with him. He was happy to oblige, and Kurt took them over there.

After that, Kurt disappeared most days after work, often for most of the evening. I became as desperate and depressed as I had been in Los Angeles years ago. I was in love with a man who had lied to me, who had not left his wife and child and who was now living a double life. I felt utterly betrayed and devastated. I would confront him, he would deny any involvement with his wife, we would shout at one another, and then I would lie awake for most of the night, torn between passion for him and rage at his behaviour.

My mental and physical health deteriorated, I was exhausted and unable to concentrate, and my business began to suffer as a result. I held it together, just about, but I could see the worried expressions on the faces of those closest to me, especially Martin, and the ripple effect was spreading through our normally happy and buzzy workplace.

I knew I had to do something, so I phoned a psychologist friend of mine, who told me to concentrate on my work and nothing else. I tried to follow his advice, but the next couple of months were very hard. Then Kurt told me his wife and daughter had left as they didn't like England. He was remorseful, and apologized for all the upset he had caused, promising to make it up to me. I was hopeful that everything would go back to normal, but it didn't. Soon after they left, he started drinking heavily and taking excessive amounts of drugs. Most days I felt that his body was there but he wasn't.

Things started to disappear from the house: silver candlesticks, photograph frames, ornaments – anything that could be sold or pawned. I knew someone was feeding a drug habit, but I didn't know if it was Kurt or Claudia's boyfriend. When I confronted them, they blamed each other. Kurt was also having psychotic incidents. He was haunted by the deaths of family members in Auschwitz and would sometimes howl in the middle of the night.

After several chaotic weeks, there came a point when I'd had enough. My feelings for him had changed almost overnight. My love for him, it seemed, had been more of an infatuation, since I now fell out of love very fast. I had been vulnerable, needy, and because of that I'd put up with a lot. But there was a limit, and our affair finally ended after an incident when he cut both his wrists and was hospitalized and then sectioned. I phoned his brother to come and rescue him.

Trying to work, suffering from heartache.

A moment of closeness with my children.

Later I heard that he had not gone back to his wife, but instead had gone to India, where he broke another heart. Many years later, he phoned and asked if he could see me. I asked him why, to which he replied, 'For the sake of memories.' I told him there were no good memories, and put the phone down.

After Kurt left, at the start of 1988, I followed my psychologist friend's advice and concentrated on work, work, work. I had let things slip during the previous chaotic months and I needed to get back on track. But almost immediately we hit a major problem with the spring/summer deliveries. Ali, our overworked pattern cutter, had relied on one of her interns to check the patterns before they were sent to the factory, and the intern had forgotten to add on enough seam allowance, which meant that many of the finished pieces were fraying at the seams. We started repairing them, but there were too many pieces and customers were screaming for delivery.

What was I to do? If I didn't send out the orders, it would mean the end of Ghost, which was unthinkable, so I decided to go ahead, reasoning that even if half were returned, we could just about survive. In fact, very few pieces were returned, but we lost a few customers who never came back. I felt bad about that, but survival was everything and I knew there were lots more customers out there.

After that, things became calmer at work and at home, and

I began to look to the future. It was time to take Ghost to the next level with a proper fashion show. Back in 1981, when I became a member of the Fashion Industry Action Group, there were only six fashion shows in London. By 1988, FIAG had become the British Fashion Council, there were more shows in London, and the BFC was doing its best to centralize and promote them under the umbrella of London Fashion Week. I wanted us to be a part of that.

We held our first Ghost runway show in March 1988 at the official London Fashion Week venue in Olympia. The show opened with four young men, the founders of cult brand Duffer of St George, gyrating their way up the runway in leather trousers and jackets, stopping at the end to do the splits. They were followed by models including Claudia and Neneh Cherry. Ty Jeffries, son of actor Lionel, made a cool entrance, and my friend Gill's children, who had performed at the Groucho Tea Party show, also showed no inhibition in dancing their way back and forth.

Halfway through the show, Ossie Clark and his dog came out and did a turn, and towards the end, my 15-year-old son William, home from school for the holidays, appeared in nothing but a pair of shorts. He danced his way delightedly along the crowded runway, but I was horrified. Who had decided to send him out like that? We didn't have a stylist; it was just me, Andrea and a couple of the others putting the outfits together, and in the throng of people backstage I hadn't seen William's outfit – or lack of one. Finally, after the obligatory long white bride's dress to mark the finale, everyone came out dancing. There was such a crowd of people on the runway that Andrea couldn't get through to the front of the stage to receive the acclaim she deserved.

The show lasted half an hour, far too long, but it was a wonderful, exuberant and chaotic success, with plenty of fun, laughter and dancing. The clothes were outstanding; Andrea had excelled. As well as the introduction of leather, there was seersucker, lace, georgette and lots of quilted jackets and coats in crepe and satin. Plus, in a major development, all of our signature pieces were in colour. After experimenting with different dyes in our kitchen at Ghost, we had discovered that direct dyes resulted in much softer hues than the strong, brittle colours produced by the reactive dyes used commercially. Reactive dyes include chemical fixatives, which mean the colours will not fade or wash out, while direct dyes have no fixative and are gentler, softer and more likely to fade. We asked Stevenson's to use direct dyes, and the result was muted, soft shades of red and purple, grey and beige.

We all felt on a high after the show. It was our first proper runway show, and although it had an amateur feel about it – the runway was too short, there wasn't enough seating and the show itself was a riot – it was exciting to be one of the companies taking part in London Fashion Week. And judging by the volume of orders that followed, we'd managed to make wearable clothing that looked as good on men and children as on women. In the back of my mind I entertained fantasies of one day launching Ghostman and Ghostkids.

In the summer of 1988, William left his boarding school with a clutch of GCSEs and came back to live with me to do his A levels at a local tutorial college. Meanwhile, in spite of spending every night out watching bands, Claudia miraculously passed her A levels, after which she announced that she was leaving home with her boyfriend to try her luck in the music business.

William and I got on really well. He would bring home one girlfriend after another for me to vet, and sometimes we had parties together. I don't know who got more drunk, him or me. I definitely wasn't a good influence and did not behave as a mother should.

I have been haunted for many years by my behaviour in regard to my children. I believe I was as good a mother as I could be, given our circumstances, until my own mother died when Claudia was six and William four. This was when I started drinking heavily. I leaned on my poor daughter, who was much too young to understand the grief I was going through. Later, when my immediate grief had turned to anger and a desire to fight the world, I wasn't there for either of them emotionally, even though I loved them deeply. They ate well, and were clean and tidy, and I usually got them to school on time, but my business consumed me and I had no idea what either of them was going through inside. I have been dealing with the guilt and shame I feel for this period since I gave up alcohol and drugs twenty years ago. I had felt abandoned by my mother as a small child, and they in turn must have felt abandoned by theirs.

I continued to blame Michael and the forced separation of the children for all the wrongs in our family. Looking back, I can see that my emotional immaturity simply provided a fertile environment for chaos at home, where children who craved security, love and consistency had limited access to these things. I don't know. Perhaps I'm being hard on myself. Or perhaps I can now see where I went wrong. Hindsight is a wonderful thing. I'm just eternally grateful that despite the failings of the past, today I have a strong, close relationship with both of my children.

In September 1988, we showed our spring/summer collection for 1989. This show was important, after the faulty orders from the previous season. The collection was a riot of multicoloured, asymmetric, flowing layers, beachwear and three-quarter-length trousers, and as before, we included some male models to show how unisex our clothes could be. The show was slightly more professional than the last, although the runway was still too short and the photographers who surrounded it perched their equipment on the edges, making it hard for the models to walk and the audience to see.

Both this show and the previous one were part of a learning curve for me. I realized that the models and outfits were only part of the show – albeit the main component – just as the script and actors are only part of a film. The truly professional shows had a theme, with casting, music, make-up, hair and accessories all coming together to make a cohesive statement. If I wanted to go further, I would need to bring on board the very best stylists, hairdressers and make-up artists. I also needed someone to produce the show, putting all the elements together. If we wanted to get press, which in turn would bring in more orders and grow Ghost, good shows were vital to our business.

By the autumn of 1989, I still hadn't found the team I needed, but we had our best show to date in terms of fashion and atmosphere. It began with a slightly twenties American feel, to the music of Benny Goodman's signature piece, 'Sing, Sing, Sing'. The models, including a bright young star in the making named Naomi Campbell, came out in white drop-waist dresses and shorts. The mood then changed to fluttering geisha girls in long embroidered kimonos over wide trousers, all shyly covering their faces with fans. Finally, in complete contrast, came a trip to Jamaica, with shorts, tops, loose cover-ups and various kinds of headwear in a sea of bright oranges, blues and the Jamaican national colours of yellow and green. The girls started dancing to reggae music, everyone backstage came out, and the runway became a noisy nightclub. My lovely friend James Lebon, a video director and graphic artist, who left this planet far too early, wound in and out of the runway crowd, pretending to film the onstage party. Once again Andrea got lost trying to get to the front to take her bow.

It was quite mad and a huge success. We had some excellent press coverage and our turnover increased from £1 million – where we had been for the past two years – to £1.5 million. In the UK we were selling to Harrods and a few of the best boutiques in and outside London. In Amsterdam we had an exclusive customer who spent £100,000 per season, and in Scandinavia a wholesaler who spent almost as much. We were selling in the States too, in Los Angeles, New York and Detroit. The buyers from these cities were exceptional in that they came to Europe to buy, and they had started to take an interest in London Fashion Week, even though it was the poor relation to Paris and Milan. International press and buyers were generally scarce on the ground in London. French and German buyers were not to be seen, although in the case of the French, Ghost had little appeal. Our collars did not stand up! We lacked structure in our clothes!

I wondered how long it would take for the British Fashion Council to get itself together and seriously promote the industry. When would they put pressure on the show organizers to up their game and provide a long runway, proper lighting, a purpose-built area for the photographers and clear information for designers who were showing?

I complained, and I'm sure others did too. Eventually the organizers decided, in their wisdom, to construct a much wider runway, rather than a longer one, which meant that for the autumn 1990 show, the models walked diagonally rather than straight. I didn't like this runway, but although I still didn't have the production team I wanted, I did like our show. I'd decided to get more serious, so we had no men or children and there was less chaos on the runway. The huge faux-fur coats we made looked wonderful over long, flimsy frilly dresses, and at the end Andrea was able to come out and take a bow without having to fight her way through a crowd.

Ghost was doing well and our figures were improving, but I was always thinking about our next step and what we might try. I had met a young American designer, James Logerfo, whose work I really liked, so I decided to try something that wasn't all about loose-fitting, flowing, bias-cut viscose. James's designs were young and sexy and totally opposite to ours in style and fabric. He liked using shiny, stretchy fabrics that clung to the body. He was looking for work and was also an experienced pattern cutter, so I asked him to join Ghost and decided to give him his own section, Spirit of Ghost, in our next show.

This might have caused an issue with the main designer at other brands, but it didn't worry Andrea, since she had other commitments and her visits were few and far between. We went ahead with designs from both James and Andrea for the next show, winter 1990, and at the end, they came out together to take a bow. However, James's clothes did not sell well and his stay at Ghost was short-lived. I had tried to do something different with him, but it hadn't worked. My customers didn't want young, rock'n'roll outfits; they wanted functional, comfortable fashion with an edge. They loved and lived in Ghost, and not in sexy body-hugging clothes.

I was proud of what we produced, but I was also frustrated. Ghost was not regarded as a real fashion house. It was seen by the press and style gurus as a middle-of-the-road label that women liked to wear. I had ambitions for us to be accepted as a brand credible to magazines like *Vogue* and *Vanity Fair*.

Perhaps it was because I had felt like an outsider all my life that it mattered to me to be an insider, accepted as part of the fashion world. In spite of having achieved a degree of financial security, built up a business from virtually nothing and given the women who wore my clothes satisfaction and pleasure, it still wasn't enough for me. I was determined to elevate the status of Ghost on the international stage.

Kate Moss modelling Ghost's summer collection, 1995.

Chapter Ten

Time to Get Serious

———

Sherald Lamden, or Sherry as she was known, was a very beautiful young woman, tall, slender and with long black hair. I first met her in the seventies at one of Harry's parties. I didn't see her again for a decade, until I met her at one of the Paris trade fairs, where she was modelling on a stand. We got talking and she told me she was helping out her boyfriend, whose company it was, by showing his designs.

We became friends, and she told me that despite plenty of requests for her to model, her real interest lay in the more creative side of fashion: styling and show production. A year later, she was sitting around a table with John Galliano, discussing how his show should look.

A fashion show producer works with the designer and the stylist on the theme, the music, the lighting, the cast and the models' hair, make-up and accessories. He or she decides the order in which the models make their entrance and tells them what impression they need to give, how they should walk and how long to pose at the end of the runway for the photographers. In other words, the entire runway show production is in the producer's hands.

All the shows we had done to date were enormous fun and full of energy, but they were not regarded as proper fashion shows and we were not being taken seriously by the fashion press. If I wanted Ghost to become a recognized brand, I needed to commit a proper budget, which would allow us to work with an experienced producer and their team to deliver a quality show.

Until now, we couldn't have afforded it, but we now had the funds, so I called Sherry and she agreed to come on board with her partner Ken Flanagan. They brought in a brilliant stylist called Debbi Mason. She was striking in both appearance and personality, and I confess that initially I was a little bit frightened of her. Debbi, like Sherry and Ken, understood the slightly eccentric, hippy Notting Hill vibe of Ghost. Debbi introduced me to Sam McKnight, who is still one of the top creative hair stylists in his field, and Mary Greenwell, one of the best make-up artists. Sherry also brought in her friend Laurence Passera, whose distinctive and emotive music provided the perfect backdrop for our shows. I now had what

I had been missing and looking for since Ghost started doing shows: a great professional team to take us to the next level.

I learned from Sherry that in order to be taken seriously, we had to make special pieces for the shows. She explained that many of the outfits top designers showed were not the pieces they sold, since the shows largely existed to enhance the image necessary to build a brand and attract the press. The public, she said, wanted to buy into a brand. I understood the logic, but I didn't like it. I wanted to show the clothes we were selling. But if I wanted Ghost to be seen as a credible fashion label, I needed to follow her advice, so I made a few special pieces for the next show, including hand-embroidered evening wear that would have been impossible to produce in volume.

The first show my new team produced was in September 1991, presenting the collection for spring and summer 1992. When I explained to Debbi that Ghost's defining concept was that it was for women of all shapes and sizes, she replied, 'Great, let's have some pregnant women in the show.' I don't know where she found them, but halfway through proceedings, six beautiful, heavily pregnant women made their entrance in multicoloured layers of shorts, tops and loose cover-ups. It was wonderful, and the applause was louder than I had ever heard at a fashion show. For the finale, a very pregnant bride sashayed down the runway in a full white dress. No one, to the best of my knowledge had ever included pregnant women in a fashion show, and I am proud that in a world of super-skinny models we dared to do it. With this show we raised our profile not only by including pregnant women, but also because Sherry, Ken and Debbi brought in top models, among them Cecilia Chancellor and Yasmin Le Bon, who were happy to take payment in clothes.

Three months later, as 1991 drew to a close, I was invited to a big New Year's Eve party at Hook End Manor, a recording studio in the Oxfordshire countryside. I checked into a nearby hotel with Woofy, who couldn't be left at home alone. Once I'd put on a lovely Ghost dress – I rarely wore anything else – and done my hair and make-up, I sprinkled a little glitter on Woofy's fur, tied a big red bow tie around his neck and off we went.

The hostess wasn't too pleased about me arriving with a dog, but Woofy wasn't keen on crowds of people, so he very considerately went and hid himself in a corner out of everyone's way. All went well until, deep into the night, an extremely drunk woman fell on top of him, and he retaliated with a slight nip. He didn't hurt her, but he was in disgrace and so was I. Woofy was the gentlest dog and he only nipped because he was snoozing quietly, bothering nobody and hardly expecting someone to drunkenly collapse on him. Now I was being asked to remove him, and of course I was upset. I was leaning over a trembling Woofy, stroking him, when a voice behind me said:

'Are you all right? Can I help in any way?'

A little jolt of lightning went through me. I knew that voice – warm and melodic and unforgettable. I turned to see a man I had met briefly two months earlier. I had been with friends in a restaurant when I'd spotted some people I knew at another table. We all left at the same time, and as I was going to the Groucho Club, I asked if anyone needed a lift to the West End. Clive Langer, one of the other group, said yes, he was going to the 100 Club, and would I mind taking his friend too?

In the car, Clive sat next to me, and his friend, a man with glasses and curly brown hair, sat in the back. As I drove and the three of us talked, I fell in love with the beautiful voice of the man behind me. I was sorry when we arrived and they thanked me and disappeared.

Now here he was, the man with the curly hair and glasses – and that voice. He introduced himself as Andrew, got me a drink and reassured me that the poor dog was perfectly within his rights to be aggrieved at a drunk woman toppling onto him. He made me laugh, and when he offered to see me back to my hotel, I happily accepted.

We talked all night in my hotel room. I must have fallen

asleep at some point, and when I woke up, he was gone. But I knew something extraordinary had begun between us.

Andrew was a drummer. He had played for artists like Sandie Shaw, Bucks Fizz and Peter Gabriel, and on Morrissey's first three solo albums after the Smiths split in 1987, *Viva Hate*, *Bona Drag* and *Kill Uncle*. Work was hectic for both of us, and to add to the complications, Andrew had a girlfriend at this time, so over the next few months we only managed a few wonderful dinners together. I knew his girlfriend wouldn't last and I waited patiently.

In February 1992, we had our best show to date. Debbi excelled herself. The mood was somewhere between Robin Hood and Pre-Raphaelite, with lots of velvet in all the colours of the forest. The models had thin black bands woven into their hair and around their foreheads, and we made long boots by wrapping suede around the models' legs and criss-crossing it with braid to keep it in place. This time Kate Moss and Saffron Burrows sashayed down the runway to the sounds of Simon & Garfunkel's 'Scarborough Fair'. It was an emotional show for me, and one that I will always remember, because at the end, for the first time and feeling extremely shy, I came out with Andrea to take a bow. Lynne Franks had told me I had to come out since Andrea was hardly ever in the country and the press needed someone they could recognize and interview.

Me and Andrew on a dinner date.

We did one more show in the official venue, in September 1992 for spring/summer 1993. It was another Debbi Mason coup; colourful, pretty, dreamy and very boho. Naomi Campbell and Susie Bick floated down the runway to Marianne Faithfull's 'The Ballad of Lucy Jordan'. Marianne's distinctive voice bemoaning that 'At the age of thirty-seven / She realized she'd never / Ride through Paris in a sports car / With the warm wind in her hair'. The next morning, half the front page of *The Times* was devoted to a photo of Naomi in our show. Finally, some real recognition. I was thrilled. We were on our way.

Shortly before the show, I invited Andrew to spend the weekend with me in Ramsgate. As we walked along the beach and talked into the night, we filled in our respective stories. I discovered he had four older brothers and an adopted younger sister. He was highly intelligent, and very funny. He had been accepted at the University of Cambridge to read English, but his drumming career had taken over. We talked about so many things, and he was so knowledgeable, I was in awe. He was warm and affectionate and loving and like no one else I had ever known, and I was falling deeply in love. With the sound of waves pounding the seashore, we cemented our relationship, and I knew deep down inside of me that this was just the beginning of our life together.

As we spent more and more time together, most people were happy for us, but my father wasn't pleased about the new man in my life. He said it would never work because Andrew was 15 years younger than I was – I was 46 and he 31 when we met. I pointed out to Dad that he himself was 15 years older than his girlfriend, but he insisted it was different. It was fine for the man to be older than the woman, but not the other way round. I proved him wrong.

The official fashion show venue was at Olympia, and it was, in my opinion, woefully inadequate. I was fed up with the lack of space for photographers, who were left to lean on the all-too-short runway, together with bad lighting and poor communication from the organizers, so I decided to move our next show, in February 1993, to the famous Café de Paris near Piccadilly Circus.

Debbi was pregnant, so she suggested that Sherry style the show as well as produce it. By this time we were all very aware of the horrible impact that the AIDS/HIV epidemic was having. Several of our friends in the fashion world had died as a result of it, including my good friend Jacques Buisson, who had been instrumental in the survival of Ghost in the early days. Lynne Franks had sent one of her employees, Janet Fischgrund, to help us. Janet and Sherry got on really well; this was the beginning of what would be a long-lasting friendship.

Both wanted to raise awareness and money for a charity that had been set up to research a cure for HIV and to help those affected. I was more than happy to agree, so we asked 30 young men and women to walk through the Café de Paris, upstairs and downstairs, wearing white T-shirts printed with the AIDS red ribbon emblem. We also had around 30 models, so it was chaotic to say the least.

First out was Jaye Davidson, the androgynous star of the BAFTA-winning film of the previous year, *The Crying Game*, dressed as a Ghost woman, twirling his cape and shawl as he walked around the café. Ossie Clark and his dog made another appearance, as did Kari-Ann Jagger, Sadie Frost, Naomi Campbell, Kate Moss and Saffron Burrows, plus 15-year-old Liberty Ross in her first ever show. Halfway through the show, model Sara Stockbridge, muse to designer Vivienne Westwood, stopped in front of Suzy Menkes of the *Herald Tribune* and Alexandra Shulman, editor of *Vogue*, and accidentally flicked cigarette ash at their feet – a moment that made my toes curl with embarrassment. My daughter came out in a voluminous yellow net skirt and a big black top hat; a very un-Ghostly outfit, but in keeping with the wisdom that runway outfits were not necessarily sales outfits and that shows were more about getting publicity to raise brand awareness.

We were proud of the show, but without Debbi's strict

professionalism we took a step backwards, presenting more as fashion entertainment than a proper runway show, though we did send out a strong message on AIDS awareness.

As always, there were very few international press or buyers present. They were a rarity at London shows, since we were a poor third to Paris and Milan, and many of those who followed fashion on the international stage just didn't bother coming to London. I felt dispirited that after all the effort we'd put in to the show, it got very little coverage.

Then came a surprise announcement – New York was going to have a fashion week. Starting from October 1993, the fashion calendar would read Paris, Milan, London and New York. The fashion press were wildly excited, and so was I; this could be our chance to do something bigger and better. Ghost already had an agency in New York, Showroom Seven. They had been helping us expand in America, and we had exhibited at a few trade shows, glamorous affairs held on two floors of the Plaza Hotel opposite Central Park. Now I was determined to make Ghost the first UK company to show at New York Fashion Week.

Showroom Seven were delighted and happy to set things in motion. Sherry and Debbi were also excited. We wanted to put together our most dazzling show, but Janet, who had done such a brilliant job as our publicist on the previous shows, had left Lynne Franks and was working for upmarket London boutique Browns. Lynne offered us another of her employees, but though capable, she was not Janet. Sherry and I decided that after the New York show we would try to tempt Janet away from Browns to be our first in-house publicist.

Meanwhile, I was facing two major headaches – both Andrea and Martin had decided to leave.

Andrea announced that she was going to get married. She had fallen in love with the man who owned the company that made Fernet-Branca, an Italian liqueur, and she wanted to have a family.

Martin, my right-hand man, also wanted to get married, and he and his new wife were going to live in Cumbria, to be near her family.

I was happy for them both, but I felt bereft. My designer and my financial rock were leaving me at the same time. How was I going to replace them? And the timing was awful: September was approaching, and the Ghost show team and I were leaving for New York in October.

I had no time to lose. Debbi introduced me to a friend of hers, a brilliant commercial designer, Angela Southwell, who had increased the turnover of several major retail shops. I liked her work and she agreed to join us. Angela, or Ange as she was known, was with us for the next three years and she designed some of our most commercial pieces, expanding our customer base and greatly increasing sales.

While Ange's strength was commercial design, we also needed original and iconic styles if Ghost was to continue gaining respect in fashion circles. I went to the MA student show at Central Saint Martins College of Fashion, where I found Sophia Malig and her graduate collection. Her talent lay in innovation, and I loved her work; she designed the kind of clothes I loved to wear. Sophia joined us and became my right hand and so much more. She was responsible for all the wonderful Ghost embroideries and fabric variations that became part of our signature.

Finding a new financial director presented a different kind of problem. I advertised, and was swamped with hundreds of replies. I narrowed it down to two and arranged to meet one of them in the West End. Andrew came with me, since I trusted his judgement. When we arrived, the would-be financial director turned to him and said, 'Your mum has a good business, hasn't she?' That was the end of the interview. I didn't need someone so tactless and thoughtless working for Ghost.

My second choice was well-qualified and seemed nice enough, so as I needed someone fast, I employed him. He came to work wearing a suit and was rather formal, which didn't fit in at all with Ghost's relaxed style. He'd been there for two weeks when I came in to find two strange men going through our books. He explained that he had brought in a couple of accountant friends to verify his fears that Ghost was overtrading – a financial term for running before you can walk. Despite my faith in Martin, I had always kept a very watchful eye on our finances, and I knew exactly where we were. Of course we were overtrading! How else could we build up the business? If I had continued at the pace this man was suggesting, it would have taken 30 years to get to where we wanted to be, and I didn't have 30 years. While we were discussing this, I noticed cheques in his drawer that he should have banked. That was it. I was furious and told him and his friends to get out.

Now I was desperate. We were leaving for New York in a couple of weeks. I phoned everyone I could think of to ask if they knew a clever young finance person who could come and help me. No one did. Just as I was on the point of giving up, I decided to phone Helen Storey, a talented designer and artist that I knew. A young man answered the phone and asked why I was calling. I explained, and he replied that he was the person I was looking for, and he would start work for me as soon as he had sorted out Helen's business and could leave it in good shape.

I didn't know whether to laugh at his self-assurance or cry with relief. I knew nothing about him, but as it turned out, he was a qualified accountant who didn't wear a suit. His name was Ris Fatah, and he fitted into Ghost like a hand into a glove and became my new rock.

I couldn't believe my luck in finding Ris and Sophia. Both of them were loyal, hard-working and brilliant and they stayed by my side for the next 13 years, until the end of Ghost as we knew it. With my team now in place, I breathed a sigh of relief. The ship was steady again.

Enjoying my 50th birthday party, 1995.

Chapter Eleven

New York

———

It never occurred to me at the time how much of a risk I was taking putting on a show in New York, but of course it could have been a complete disaster.

Fern Mallis, of the Council of Fashion Designers of America, had announced the formation of '7th on Sixth' to coordinate the shows that would mark New York's first ever fashion week on the international fashion calendar. There were two official venues offered, and I decided to show in the smaller of them, the New York Library, a landmark building in Midtown Manhattan.

Our agents in New York, Showroom Seven, had advised us to work with Alex de Betak, a French show producer based in New York. Sherry and Ken had split up after our last show, so I was pleased and relieved to have a producer who was familiar with how things worked in the city. Sherry would still be very much involved in all areas, but Alex would take charge. He was just 25 when he produced that first show for us, and he was brilliant. We didn't know it then, but he would go on to become one of the most sought-after and respected fashion show producers worldwide.

I arrived with my design team, together with Sherry and Laurence Passera – who were becoming an item – and Debbi, who had left her baby with his father for a few days. Our hair and make-up team were already there doing other shows. Karen, the head of Showroom Seven, had booked us rooms at the Gramercy Park Hotel on Lexington Avenue, just off Gramercy Park. In London it would be called a square, but in Manhattan it was a park.

Walking into the hotel, I had a strong feeling of déjà vu. It was just like the Chateau Marmont, where I had stayed on my honeymoon 24 years earlier. It had certainly seen much better days and was now somewhat dilapidated, with an aura of bohemian decadence. Although rather shabby, the rooms were huge, and I felt at home. The same kind of people who had been at the Chateau were now installed in the Gramercy: photographers, musicians, actors, artists and models. One of the photographers told me that when they departed from the hotel, they would all leave whatever drugs they had leftover behind the ledges in the corridors. It was an unwritten rule, he explained, so there would always be a little something for a returning guest.

Since we were the only British company showing in the first official New York Fashion Week, we decided to make it a very British show. The opening music, from *My Fair Lady*, was Rex Harrison shouting, 'Damn! Damn! Damn! Damn! I've grown accustomed to her face'. This was followed by a reggae version of the *Coronation Street* theme, music from Marianne Faithfull, and of course Britain's greatest ever music export to the US, the Beatles. To add a bit of humour and fun, I invited Quentin Crisp, the renowned raconteur, who at the age of 84 was still writing and performing, to make an entrance with me at the end of the show. I will never forget this wonderful petite man, who after taking a bow to rapturous applause was escorted off the runway by two models towering above him on either side.

Amazingly, most of the top models agreed to do our show, not for money but for clothes. I was overwhelmed with joy, since we couldn't possibly have afforded their rates. In London, well-known models who had done our shows had also taken payment in clothes. Now in New York we had all the supermodels: Naomi and Kate from home, Christy Turlington, Carla Bruni, Patricia Velasquez, Emma Balfour, Lucie de la Falaise, Karen Mulder and many others. The outfits we showed were in the subtle, muted colours I had painted looking out at the sea in

Me and Quentin Crisp at our first New York show, 1993.

Ramsgate. There were lots of bias cuts and the clothes literally floated down the runway. In contrast, tights had been perfectly laddered by Sophia the night before the show as part of the effect that Debbi, with Sherry's help, had styled so beautifully.

The show was a huge success; it couldn't have gone better. The next day I was invited on to *Good Morning America*, which was fast becoming the most watched morning TV show. I told the American public all about my little house in Ramsgate, how on a clear night I could see the lights in France shimmering on the other side of the pond, and where the inspiration for the colours in the collection came from.

Naomi Campbell appeared with me, and explained that if you were to ask any top model what brand they liked to wear when they weren't working, the answer was Ghost. This was confirmed by backstage film clips. Carla Bruni, who would later become the wife of French president Nicolas Sarkozy, said, 'I am taking payment in clothes.' Michele Hicks talked about how she could wear a Ghost dress with boots and a motorcycle jacket, and Tatjana Patitz said she could dress our clothes up or down. Aside from the versatility, the models also liked the fact that they could get several outfits into one small bag. Since they were constantly travelling, Ghost really served a purpose, and any creases could be smoothed out by hanging the clothes in a hot bathroom at their destination.

My whole philosophy was now a reality. I was producing versatile, feminine, functional clothes that women at the heart of the fashion world loved.

Grace Coddington, once Michael's flatmate, now fashion director of American *Vogue*, said, 'She just makes clothes that women want to wear.' I think this might have been intended to dismiss me in fashion circles, but it was music to my ears.

Ghost's fame was further enhanced by an incident at our post-show party. It had been organized by our agents in the up-and-coming Meatpacking District of New York, and among others, The Chemical Brothers and a few Red Hot Chili Peppers came, lured by our beautiful models.

I was talking to Christy Turlington when she suddenly hunched up like a cat about to pounce. I turned to see a journalist and a photographer from one of the major British newspapers walking towards us. As they approached, Christy leapt forward and kicked the photographer in the balls, then punched him in the face. It transpired that this photographer had taken a picture of her while she was changing backstage in Paris, and the resulting shot had been published in various newspapers. Her revenge was press heaven for Ghost – it made all the papers the next day, and orders poured in.

We returned to London triumphant. Ghost was doing better than I had ever dreamed possible. Ris, who had settled in as our accountant, told me we needed a bank loan to finance the orders, which now totalled £3 million. My old friend at Barclays was happy to oblige.

What was more difficult on a day-to-day basis was consistent cash flow. A friend of mine, Chris, told me how his wife, Marion, was struggling with her shop in Hinde Street, just off Marylebone High Street. This was Marion Foale, whose wonderful designs I had saved up to buy in the sixties, when she and her friend Sally Tuffin had their shop. In the early nineties, Marion was keeping many women employed hand-knitting her beautiful wool pieces. I regarded her then, and still do now, as one of the great British designers. It saddens me that her astonishing talent has never been acknowledged by the fashion establishment.

I offered to put some sale-or-return Ghost items in Marion's shop. She agreed, and within weeks, sales were so good that we couldn't restock fast enough. Soon after this, Marion told me she wanted to give the shop up, as it was too much for her, and would I like to take it over? I said yes, and just like that, Ghost had its first retail outlet, a few minutes' walk from Selfridges. Marion continued working with her knitters, supplying some of the best shops worldwide, including Bergdorf's in New York.

In 1994, we returned to New York for the fall show and stayed in the Gramercy Park Hotel again – it was to be our home for all but one of the 13 shows we did in the city. It became an even better workplace when we were given exclusive use of the very spacious penthouse roof terrace, which we used for castings, walk-throughs and hanging out.

This time we held our show in the purpose-built tent in Bryant Park. It was perfectly and efficiently put together, incomparably better than the venues where we had shown in London. Helena Christensen and Shalom Harlow joined our model cast, and Naomi opened the show.

The feel of this show borrowed something from Christian Dior's ultra-feminine New Look, introduced in 1947, when his cinched-in waists and full skirts took the fashion world by storm. We combined this with Ghost's signature bias cuts and asymmetry. Kate Moss captured all the press shots by appearing in a voluminous cream quilt jacket, draped off her shoulders, over a short bias-cut dress in muted shades of pink, to the sound of Doris Day singing 'Perhaps, Perhaps, Perhaps'.

At the end of the show, I came out onto the runway, feeling very shy. It was the first time I had appeared on my own. Ghost was no longer a ghost. It had a face and a body – mine. I was having to get used to being in the spotlight. And while I didn't think our second show quite equalled the excitement or originality of the first, it did mark a turning point. Ghost was now an established fixture in New York Fashion Week.

Back in London, it was time to get ready for our annual Christmas sale, which was becoming more and more popular. There was no social media then, but there was no need for it. It's amazing how fast word of mouth can spread. In the years to come, our Christmas sale would be attended by thousands and came to represent 10 per cent of our turnover.

Once the sale was over and 1995 had been ushered in, it was time to celebrate Claudia's twenty-fifth birthday and my fiftieth. We hired a large venue off Gloucester Road, and I made fish pies and salads for two hundred people with the help of Claudia and a wonderful Portuguese assistant. I have no idea why I didn't use a catering company; it just didn't occur to me, or maybe I'm a masochist.

The birthday cake was provided by my good friend, architect and interior designer Ted Walters, his wife Willie, who was a senior lecturer in women's wear at Central Saint Martins, Suggs from Madness and his wife Anne (whose stage name was Bette Bright). It was in the shape of my dog Woofy, and while the resemblance was questionable, it was the loveliest gesture.

Most of the Ghosties, as I liked to call my staff, came to the party, as did various celebrities. Ossie Clark managed to make a scene by throwing fish pie at an innocent bystander. He also brought a dress he had made for me, and insisted I put it on.

It was a creamy colour, figure-hugging and structured with lots of bone, making it extremely uncomfortable, although beautiful to look at. It was a memorable and fun party, but very early the next morning Ossie came round, banging on the front door and demanding £2,000 for the dress, which I had thought was a birthday present. I wouldn't let him in, and he kept shouting in the street. Finally I threw the dress out of the window and told him to keep it. He must have given it back to me at some point, since it is still hanging in my wardrobe.

My present to myself for reaching the age of 50 was a facelift. All my female relatives had been very jowly, and I was no exception. After doing some research with the help of *Vogue*'s beauty editor, I settled on a plastic surgeon who operated on me in the Wellington Hospital. Afterwards I had to sleep upright for a week, and when the bandages were removed my face was black and blue. I was miserable and in pain, and everywhere I went I got pitying looks from people who assumed I was the subject of physical abuse. I wrote an article for *Vogue* entitled 'My face does not belong to me', in which I concluded that I could have got the same result by dieting, exercising and giving up alcohol. The surgery made a little difference, but not enough to compensate for the unpleasantness I suffered. I trust that plastic surgery has improved since then.

Of all the shows we did in New York, there are two that

really stand out for me. The first of these took place late in 1995. New York Fashion Week had grown so fast that by this time there were lots of designers showing in the Bryant Park official venue. I'm not sure whether I wanted Ghost to be different or whether I wanted an event rather than a succession of outfits, but I decided we would show somewhere else. I asked Karen, our American agent, to find out how much it would cost to hire the Oyster Bar, a vast, cavernous restaurant in Grand Central Station. It was large enough for our purposes and close to the official venue. Karen came back with a ridiculous figure in the region of $120,000. I phoned the Oyster Bar and asked how much it would cost to have a dinner party for 500 people. They quoted me $36,000 to hire the bar and provide dinner. I jumped at it, and then got Karen to ask her friend, actor and comedian Sandra Bernhard, if she would narrate the show.

It was an ambitious and difficult project, and we encountered all sorts of problems. There wasn't enough power in the restaurant for our lights, so we had to dig down and install cables, for which we needed various permissions. It was a nightmare, but well worth it. During the show, the newly formed fashion police – a small group of the Muslim Brotherhood who hired themselves out as a security detail to fashion agencies and venues – patrolled outside to stop any curious passers-by or fashion fans trying to get in.

Sandra was sardonic and funny. She opened the show by telling the audience to get over themselves: 'Good evening, ladies and gentlemen, welcome to the fabulous Oyster Bar. You all look so glamorous, so jaded, so fed up with fashion. Well, get over it. Get into a new mood. Lift yourself up emotionally, psychically, physically. Get out of your doldrums. Do not be bitter. You've never seen this before. This is Ghost Autumn/ Winter 1995/1996 and on into the Millennium.'

The look for this show stepped away from our usual flowing, loose-layered outfits. Our clothes were sophisticated, structured and glamorous, with lots of velvet and fake fur.

The event was packed to the brim with the world's most gorgeous models, including new young British models Jodie Kidd and Stella Tennant, but Sandra stole the show. She called fake fur 'phoney pony' and claimed that the model Chandra North's parents were 'so drunk they couldn't say Sandra'. The models all played along, sitting on tables and interacting with the audience. It was a wonderful show, edgy and improvised; something that would be difficult to pull off today.

The other show that really stands out for me was the one we held the following year, the Store Wars show.

Charivari was one of the first US stores to buy Ghost. Barbara Weiser and her brother Jon ran the five New York outlets, which had been founded by their mother, Selma, who

Oyster Bar show – celebrating with models.

had since retired. Charivari had been the first to introduce European labels to the American market and had been extremely successful. It championed avant-garde design and was one of the go-to places for cutting-edge fashion in New York. However, by the mid-nineties it had fierce competition, not least from the store chain Barneys. I had met one of the owners of Barneys after our last show, and she had told me in a heavy drawl that she was going to put me on the map 'from the east coast to the west coast'. I didn't take to her, whereas I had become friends with Barbara and in the previous year had been getting frantic phone calls from her. She told me that the basement where Charivari's stock was kept had been flooded, not to mention all sorts of other inexplicable disasters. This gave me the inspiration for the title of the show.

In the autumn of 1996, we rented a cavernous disused bank in Union Square, and since the show was being held at cocktail hour, we piled the tables high with vodka and caviar – I had found a black-market source of excellent and surprisingly inexpensive Russian beluga caviar.

We opened with the music from *Star Wars*, and dressed the models as warriors with elaborate headpieces. It was unconventional and exciting and was attended by plenty of celebrities from the film, music and fashion worlds. I was more than flattered when, a few years later, the extraordinary Alexander McQueen, who by then was chief designer at Givenchy, told me how much he had enjoyed and been inspired by this show.

New York Fashion Week was the last in the fashion calendar at this point, and we had shown Store Wars at the end of October, so we decided our after-show party should have a Halloween theme. We hired the Gentleman's Club, off Wall Street, and did our best to keep the venue a secret until the last minute. Our parties were such a hot ticket that it had become a challenge for fashion fans to gatecrash them, not least because of the certainty that celebrities like Leonardo DiCaprio and Brad Pitt would be there. We would wait until the end of the show before giving out invitations, but even then, fashion fans would get hold of one and rush to Kinko's 'we never close' printers to have them copied. This time, to prevent counterfeits, we designed and had made a very special invitation. It was a green cut-out horned Halloween mask, printed on the inside with the words 'No admission without this invite' and impossible to copy at short notice.

The party was a lavish affair. Ris had gone to Coney Island and hired a fortune teller, plus an illustrated man, a bearded lady, and a snake charmer, complete with an albino snake.

I arrived fairly early, and was standing near the entrance

when a couple strolled up. The invitation masks were supposed to be worn, making it simple for the doorman to identify legitimate guests. But this couple had no masks. I asked them where their invitations were, and the woman replied that they had given them to their cab driver.

Now I was angry. 'If that's how little you think of our invitation, which clearly states that you need it to be admitted, then I think you had better leave,' I said haughtily.

At this point I became aware of several paparazzi closing in on us. Karen, our agent, made wild signs at me before rushing over to whisper in my ear, 'Don't you know who she is? That's Sofia Coppola.' Sofia had not made her directorial debut at this point, though she had appeared in *The Godfather*. However, this didn't make her a celebrity in my eyes. I turned to her and said icily, 'So you're famous by association?'

I don't know to this day if Sofia and her partner stayed or left, although I'm sure they received abject apologies. I was hurried away by Karen and my press people, but they should have thanked me, because my altercation with the daughter of legendary film director Francis Ford Coppola ensured that our party was featured in every newspaper the next day. It was definitely our most spectacular event in New York, and marked the point where Ghost became known as much for its parties as its fashion shows.

Susanne Deeken and me talking to Princess Anne during
her visit to Ghost, 1998.

Chapter Twelve

Flying

———

My relationship with Andrew had become much more than simply an affair. He gave me the stability and support I needed at a time when I could have buckled under the weight of the demands of running a business.

He had left his flat in Battersea to come and live with me in Kensal Road. The house was more spacious since I had bought a flat next door and, with Ted overseeing things, we had connected the two.

Both my children, now in their twenties, were living at home again. Claudia, thank goodness, had left her druggy boyfriend, and was writing music and rehearsing with her band, 12 Rounds. The ground floor of Ghost's first office in Kensal Road had become a studio for her and her fellow band members.

William had left university after just one year to join his

father in a film company making a film called *The Punk*. Michael directed and William produced it. They showed it in Cannes during the film festival, and sold it to a number of countries, but there was virtually no profit. Now William was back at home with me and was planning to film the Notting Hill Carnival, after which he wanted to open a restaurant with his friend Albert Clark, Ossie's son.

I don't think either of my children was thrilled to have a new man in their lives. It wouldn't have mattered who the new man was; they were simply used to having their mother to themselves. Andrew, for his part, didn't understand why they were still living at home. He himself had had to leave home at the age of 18, as had his older brothers. Inevitably the atmosphere was a little strained.

I explained to him that my children had gone through many trials and traumas in their lives, and I was not about to ask them to leave their home. As a compromise, I suggested that he and I move out, and I started looking for somewhere for us. I had absolutely no doubts about leaving Kensal Road and moving in with Andrew. We had been spending our weekends in Ramsgate, and it was here in the little house by the sea that we became aware that our love would last as long as we lived.

We would talk all night, and Andrew, with his analytical

brain, would give me insight into the problems and challenges I was facing with a business growing at breakneck speed. Our wonderful romantic nights were filled with music like Donald Fagen's *The Nightfly* playing in the background.

When the tide was out, we would walk to Broadstairs with Woofy to buy fresh fish. And we learned to fly. Andrew was fearful of heights, and he wanted to overcome this. I was excited and happy to learn too. We went to Manston airport, on the outskirts of Ramsgate, which had been heavily involved in the Battle of Britain. It had one of the widest and longest runways in the country and had been a major target for the Luftwaffe, which led to the local population being evacuated. Only a small percentage had returned, which explained why Ramsgate was such a quiet place . . . and why we loved it.

We learned to fly in little Cessna planes. Before taking off, we had to go through a long list of checks, none of which I now remember, since I hated this part of flying. I loved taking off and landing, but the checks really tested my patience.

I had the ridiculous notion that if I could fly, I could visit Ghost's production units, which by this time were scattered all over England, from Skegness to Leeds and beyond. It was time-consuming to go to all of them, and flying seemed to be the answer, but I had no idea until I learned to fly that there were roads in the sky. You couldn't simply go from A to B; you had first to go to C and possibly D, so it was never going to work as I had imagined it would, even if I'd been able to take my flying to the next level.

After 40 hours with an instructor, I was allowed to fly solo. I will always remember my first solo flight. I had flown around the bay and was preparing to land when a voice with a strong accent came over my radio saying, 'Alpha Lima, hold on Pegwell Bay.' I didn't understand the message and asked the tower to repeat it. Then I realized *I* was Alpha Lima, and looking out of my window I saw an enormous jet flying straight towards me. It was one of those 'Oh shit!' moments when you feel frozen in time. Heart thudding, I sped forward out of the jet's path and watched it swoop down to the runway as I circled shakily above the bay.

In order to get my private pilot's licence, I had to make forced landings and forward and sideway spins. This was several steps too far for me, but Andrew went all the way and got his licence. My flying was good enough for me to be co-pilot, though, and we sometimes hired a little Cessna and flew to Le Touquet on the French coast at weekends, where there was a Michelin-starred restaurant. It was fun and took me away from designs, patterns, production and business for a short time.

A friend told me that Katrine Boorman, who was one half of a DJ duo called the Cleavage Sisters, was selling the flat she had moved to after separating from Tom Conran. It was within walking distance of Kensal Road, and turned out to be two thirds of an old Victorian house with a garden. It was perfect for us. I sold the little apartment I had bought adjoining the main house in Kensal Road to DJ and musician Jeremy Healy, and we moved. However, we were driven mad by the noisy tenants above us, so Andrew sold his flat in Battersea and we bought them out. Once we had the whole house, we put in a sound studio for Andrew where he could work.

After my unhappy affair with Kurt, I had continued drinking and using cocaine. It was the fuel that gave me the energy to function on not very much sleep, and by and large it worked. Happy as I was with Andrew, work was hugely demanding, and I told myself that my drink and drug habit enabled me to cope and was under control. I knew it wasn't a good way to be living, but I needed the crutch. Andrew didn't like what I was doing, but I wasn't willing to talk about stopping.

Ghost was growing so fast that a design team rather than a single designer was becoming a necessity. Debbi and her husband had decided to make New York their home, and Ange was going to have another baby, so they had both left. Sophia had her hands full with fabrics, embroidery designs, and fittings, and the collections needed greater depth and breadth.

Enter designers Susanne Deeken and Nicholas Knightly, and stylist Alister Mackie. I don't know whether I was a good judge of brilliance or simply lucky – perhaps a little of both – but all three of them went on to have spectacular careers.

Susanne had graduated from Central Saint Martins in 1995, and Nicholas in 1993. After Ghost, Susanne went on to design for many major labels, including Marc Jacobs, Ungaro and Valentino, before turning her talents to film-making, while Nicholas went on to save Mulberry before becoming leather goods design director at Louis Vuitton.

Alister, another young graduate from Central Saint Martins, had worked on the very hip magazine *Dazed & Confused*, and I was flattered when he agreed to become our stylist. Debbi's slightly boho look needed a light refresh, and Alister provided this, adding wit and sophistication. He would go on to become creative director of *Another Man* and a world-class fashion stylist.

On the music front, Laurence Passera, who had given our early shows such energy, fun and rhythm – except where I had insisted on a little *My Fair Lady* and Doris Day – decided to pursue a career in photography. Jeremy Healy, the DJ who had bought my flat in Kensal Road, normally only scored John Galliano shows, but he agreed to score one show for us while we looked for someone to replace Laurence.

Janet Fischgrund had, much to my delight, left Browns to become our publicist. I knew that her boyfriend, James Lavelle, was a musician who had been a pioneer of trip hop and electronica in the early nineties and had founded the Mo' Wax record label, and I asked her whether he might like to work with us. We were thrilled when he agreed, and he did most of our show music from 1996.

He recently posted the following on Facebook:

The first time I did music for fashion catwalk shows was in 1996, for London fashion house Ghost. I met Ghost's Tanya Sarne, who at the time was one of London's greatest female fashion entrepreneurs and personalities (Jennifer Saunders would base her *Absolutely Fabulous* character on her). What a truly amazing experience and education; I had never experienced a world like it, truly wild and eccentric. It was such an amazingly exciting time, where music, art and fashion came together in an explosive way.

I thanked James for this generous piece, although as I have said, I believe the main characters in *Ab Fab* were based on an amalgamation of people, including me and Lynne Franks.

With a brilliant team in place to work on our shows, which were now highly professional, beautifully crafted and original,

I could get on with what mattered most – making sure that every collection was as good as it could possibly be. I had little time for anything else, because I was always hands-on, checking that we had the right balance of items in each collection and that every piece was both beautiful and comfortable.

Sophia generally did the line sheets. These were given to buyers when they were shown the collection. Each page concentrated on a fabric, with little sketches of every piece in that fabric and the price of each piece. I would go over them initially and scribble comments on them, like 'why are there two summer coats and not one shirt?', 'if we are using drill where are the trousers?', 'the silhouette is too straight, this does not make it easy, just dull, if our silhouette and bust lines don't change, we're dead', 'this section should be lace trim, where is it?'

I wanted every piece to be flattering, so I would be present at every fitting and would note down my comments: 'too long in the body above the waist', 'too much separation between the breasts', and so on. I also did the odd design sketch, which subsequently had to be redone by someone who could draw well enough to make sense to the pattern cutter.

I gave lectures to my sales team. Ghost was a mix-and-match, machine-washable designer collection. Even existing long-term customers needed to be reminded that all our fabrics were unique because of our production process, which included original embroideries by Sophia and original colours painted by me in Ramsgate. First-time buyers had to be given a brief explanation and demonstration of our methods, including the boiling and dyeing, so that they understood their orders would not be delivered with uniform size, fit or colour.

The sales team also had to point out that all the fabrics would have natural stretch to accommodate different body shapes, every style was available in any of the ten different colours we offered every season, and every garment was machine-washable, could be tumble dried and did not need ironing. I suggested they introduce the colours in a certain order. For instance, for the 1996 spring/summer collection, they should start with midnight, followed by cloud, fuchsia, peat, samphire, petrol, camel, berry, black and white.

By this time we had 294 customers in 32 countries. In America we were selling in 30 states to 92 customers. The UK came second with 56 customers, followed by Spain and Italy.

In 1998, we heard that we had won the UK Fashion and Textile Export Award. It was a great feeling to have some recognition for all our hard work, even if it was for the business side rather than the creative side. And while I would have loved it to be a design award, I was still thrilled. I went along with Ris to a glamorous lunch at the Grosvenor House Hotel off Park

Lane, where we were presented with the award, an inscribed perspex block, by Princess Anne. When we returned to work and held the award aloft, the whole staff cheered. We put it on display, and it gave us all a glow. Princess Anne paid us a visit a short time after the award ceremony and met all the staff, who didn't know whether to curtsey or bow.

In London, the shop we had taken over from Marion Foale in Marylebone was doing so well that we decided to open another one closer to our headquarters. At that point all the traditional antique shops in the Westbourne Grove and Portobello Road area of Notting Hill were disappearing and the area was buzzing with new energy. The first organic health food shop, Whole Foods, had opened, along with various fashion and luxury goods shops. It seemed like the right area for Ghost, so we looked around and found a shop for rent in Ledbury Road, just off Westbourne Grove. It had originally been a fish and chip shop and then an antiques shop, and it was perfect. We signed the lease and left it to Ted Walters to transform it into a beautiful environment where women would enjoy shopping. He bought big Venetian mirrors in the flea market in Paris – these were to become a feature of all our shops, and created an atmosphere that was warm, comfortable, feminine and spacious; each changing room was large enough to accommodate a vintage leather armchair. I was delighted with the end result.

We now had two shops, which was good for our visibility and our cash flow. But inevitably it also meant more to think about. Staff had to be hired, and Ris, who was always thinking about expansion and making more money, asked me to consider accessories like bags, shoes and even cushion covers and quilts. This seemed a step too far, given my huge workload, but I asked Sophia to do some research.

Goodness knows why, since I was already working 12-plus hours a day, but at this point I agreed to help Sherry and our publicist Janet put together their own collection. Sherry, who was a brilliant producer and stylist, had always wanted to do her own range, and watching me dismiss various fabrics I was shown by salespeople inspired her. My staff weren't happy – they had enough to do producing Ghost – but I cajoled them and they rose to it. Sherry and Janet's collection was called Seraph, and they produced two great shows, one of them in the original Wagamama, then a new restaurant in Bloomsbury.

Seraph was a young, fun collection, almost all close-fitting, simple and inexpensive, and it was a big success with the fashion press. However, production was putting too much of a strain on the Ghost staff, so Janet and Sherry got a grant from the government and moved their collection to another home, where it continued for another few years until they went in different directions and called it a day.

When Janet left us in May 1997 to work with Sherry full-time, her assistant, Alex Barlow, took over. Alex was lovely. She had joined us in 1994 straight from university and I'd made her my personal assistant until we moved her over to work with Janet and learn the PR ropes. She took to her new role brilliantly and stayed on as our PR director for the next five years.

Sometime before we started producing Seraph, I'd had a call from Sheilagh Brown, a talented designer who had taken over as the head of women's wear design at Marks & Spencer. I had met her before; she and Tessa, my second partner at Miz, had been at the Royal College of Art at the same time and had become friends.

Sheilagh invited me to her office to discuss doing a collection for Marks. I was dubious, since I thought it might affect our UK business, but Sheilagh said the items would be marketed as M&S clothes and our name wouldn't appear on them, which reassured me. I agreed to a very limited collection of a dress, a pair of trousers, a top and a jacket. I was told that Coats Viyella, Marks's long-term production partner, would produce the garments and Ghost would receive 3 per cent of the wholesale price. It seemed like very little return, but since it involved virtually no work for us, I agreed. We modified a few existing pieces and handed them over. I knew we wouldn't see the results for at least a year, but I confess to being a little excited to see how it would work out.

Shortly after Seraph moved out of Ghost, the Marks & Spencer royalties began coming in, and they exceeded any expectations we might have had. The dress we had given them was one of their best-selling dresses since the war, and the trousers sold close to half a million pairs. I wanted to keep the royalties separate from the Ghost income, so I opened another bank account in the name of my dog, Woofy.

Our collaboration with M&S continued for the next few years. Every year we would give them a limited range of new designs, and they did extremely well and added to our Woofy account. Even when Sheilagh left for another job, the arrangement carried on.

We now employed 30 people at Ghost HQ, and 6 in the 2 shops. The atmosphere in our HQ was buzzy and energetic; we all worked incredibly hard and we were like a family. I still had lunch made for everyone every day, and every summer I hired a coach and we went on a day trip to Ramsgate. A couple of the staff would put on little frilly aprons and serve champagne with orange juice and croissants on the way. Once there, everyone changed at my house before going to the beach. We spent the day playing rounders and volleyball, drank lots of wine and cold beer and had a barbecue. It was

Ghost in Ramsgate, 1996, as featured on that year's Christmas card.

great fun and it brought us all together, as did the warehouse sale at Christmas.

This had started as a three-day event but had grown to four. We opened the doors at 11 am, but an hour before that there were already long queues. The sale had become incredibly popular, and I was touched when Ruth Picardie, a journalist who was writing a column in the *Observer* about her cancer journey, talked about how sad she would be if she missed it.

The Christmas sale not only helped our cash flow; it also made it possible for the staff to have an annual bonus. To quote Sir Edwin Hardy Amies, 'I was clever. I knew that I had to put together the best team and look after them.'

Our sales each year were now close to £5 million. While this was impressive, our net profits weren't vast, because to keep prices affordable, we only ever doubled our cost price, so if a garment cost us £25 to make, we sold it for £50. We also had to write off around 3 per cent of our clothes to damage because of our very intensive production process, which was the reason companies trying to copy us so often gave up.

Our retail sales boosted profits. Retail outlets would mark up by 2.7 times their cost price, meaning that the piece we sold for £50 would cost £135 in a shop. If the shops were ours, this profit was even greater. This was one of the reasons why we decided to open another shop, but there was a second reason, and that was brand image. Known names like Dior and Chanel had flagship shops around the world. These were intended to maintain their image as much as to make money. I wanted Ghost to be known as a brand in the same way, and since we already had two shops in London, we looked at our markets abroad. California was perfect for Ghost; our summery style suited the weather. It was a bold move, but it felt right – we would open our next shop in Los Angeles.

Me and Amanda Donohoe standing outside our LA shop.

Photograph taken by Andrew Macpherson.

Chapter Thirteen

Expansion

I was nervous about returning to LA after my experiences there in the late sixties. The place held nothing but bad memories for me. However, whereas in 1969 I had been appalled by all the drug-taking, in 1998 my own cocaine habit made me fearless.

I stayed with my long-time friend, actress Amanda Donohoe, who had moved to LA for her acting career, and set out to scout for shops.

Robertson Boulevard, at right angles to Sunset Boulevard and Santa Monica, was becoming a very fashionable district. Opposite the Newsroom Café and almost next door to the Ivy, the chic West Hollywood restaurant where all the major celebrities lunched and dined, was a vast empty glass-fronted shop. It looked far too large and glamorous for Ghost, but in LA everything seemed larger than life, and cute little shops just didn't stand out, so I made enquiries. It seemed there was heavy competition for this property, and a French company was about to sign the lease.

Undaunted, I found out who the owners were and approached them. Don and Phyllis Epstein were a delightful elderly couple; it would have been difficult to find more genteel and sophisticated people in the whole of LA. Don's family had owned the first company to import modern European furniture into America, and Phyllis's grandfather had invented and developed a type of refrigeration.

When we met, they asked about me and Ghost, and whether we had any references. It turned out that they were good friends with the owner of a store I had been selling to for several years and with whom I'd become friends. They contacted him and he sang my praises, which sealed the deal. The French company were furious and threatened to sue, but that never materialized. They were out and Ghost was in.

Ted Walters flew into town, checked into a hotel for a month, and went to work designing and styling our first US retail store. The plan was ambitious: a beautiful dark-wood floor, large Venetian mirrors, and chandeliers, with an emphasis on femininity and comfort. The end result was fabulous.

Finding good staff we could trust to run the store in our absence was more difficult. Most of the people we interviewed were keener on telling us how their star sign made them compatible with the job than convincing us they had any relevant experience. In the end, we had to poach staff from elsewhere. I would go into a store, spot someone who looked as though they knew what they were doing, approach them and ask if they were interested in running a brand-new outlet.

Ris and Alex flew over for the opening in June 1998. We threw a memorable party, which many celebrities attended, thanks to our new LA press agent, Marilyn Heston, actor Charlton Heston's daughter-in-law.

By the time I returned to the UK, the store was open and everything was in place. Unfortunately, even with the poached staff, things didn't always go smoothly. In our absence, they appeared to suffer under the illusion that the shop was theirs, and became very choosy about who they would sell to and who they would ignore. This became evident when we received a number of complaints from customers who felt the staff had been rude to them.

Despite my attempts to sort this out, which was always going to be difficult at a distance, the LA shop never made as much money as we thought it would. But it was fabulous for our image, attracting celebrities and their stylists, and it was instrumental in getting us a very lucrative perfume deal a couple of years later.

Since the profits from retail were so much higher than those from wholesale, Ris suggested we should open concessions in department stores, rather than selling directly to them. It made sense, so while I was in Los Angeles preparing to open the store, Ris was busy in London negotiating terms for our proposed outlets. Initially we opened in Selfridges and Harvey Nichols, and the Selfridges sales reached £1 million annually.

Fifteen years after I had started a fashion business in my kitchen, Ghost now had three shops, two concessions and a wholesale business worth several million pounds. We had doubled the staff, in a matter of months, from 30 to 60. We had already added knitwear to our collections, and our plan was to design and manufacture a range of other accessories.

After going back and forth to Los Angeles to sort out the shop, we couldn't face another trip to the States, so we decided to do our next show in London. I wanted something a little more exciting than the official venue, so I asked the Saatchi Gallery if we could show there. The gallery had been opened in 1985, in a disused paint factory in St John's Wood, by advertising agency founder and art lover Charles Saatchi. It was a beautiful, large, light space, perfect for a fashion show, and to my surprise and delight, Charles Saatchi agreed.

The show, in February 1998, was a huge success, and afterwards we joined forces with Alexander McQueen's

Show at the Saatchi Gallery for winter 1998.

team for a riotous party at the Groucho Club. I didn't know Alexander well, but we had mutual respect for one another, and as well as sharing a casting director, Sidonie, our two teams had friends in common. A few years later, my good friend Sherry would become creative director for McQueen's second collection, McQ, and Janet Fischgrund would become his publicist. I believe everyone had a fantastic evening, judging by the stories I heard over the next few days, though personally I don't remember very much, apart from my son William playing doorman and having the time of his life flirting with Kate Moss and Demi Moore.

After this show, we returned to New York. With all that was going on, I no longer had the energy or inspiration to attempt any more Oyster Bar extravaganzas, but we continued to stage successful shows in the official venue at Bryant Park, thanks to our excellent team and the big-name models who continued appearing for us in return for clothes. If I'm honest, though, New York lost its magic for us as more and more fashion companies began doing runway shows there and it became less personal and more businesslike.

In the run-up to our twelfth show, in September 1999, disaster struck when we heard that Hurricane Floyd was on its way. Our show was due to start just as the storm was predicted to be lashing Manhattan, so it was cancelled and we were told that we could show at the very end of the week instead. Since all the press, buyers and models would have left town by then, putting on a runway show at that point would be an expensive waste of our time. We scrambled to find available models who would fit the outfits we'd had made. Although they denied it, we were pretty sure that the organizers had bussed in the audience from various women's clubs so that we wouldn't have an empty tent. The whole episode left a bad taste, especially as in the end the hurricane caused very little damage and our show need not have been cancelled.

The millennium was approaching, and I planned to throw a huge party. Ted constructed an intricately scaffolded roof that covered the entire garden of our house, plus a stage and a dance floor fitted over the grass. Claudia and our friend Katrina Phillips helped decorate the inside of our custom-made marquee with the Arabian Nights as our inspiration, and invitations went out to our friends to come and 'Rock the Casbah'. Word must have spread far and wide, since on the night, politicians, actors, models, musicians and a host of others we hadn't sent invitations to turned up for the celebration. We didn't mind at all; it was a truly wonderful night and we danced until dawn and into the next day.

We kept the garden flooring and the marquee for another two weeks, as January was birthday time. Claudia, her boyfriend Atticus, William's girlfriend Samantha and I all had birthdays in mid-January, along with our good friend Suggs. This time we covered the inside walls of the marquee with velvet, and another huge bash ensued. Unfortunately, the neighbours weren't as obliging as they had been for our New Year's Eve extravaganza. After visits from the council and the police, the music was halted at midnight and the party had to continue indoors.

I had learned in the course of running Ghost that a designer working for a well-established label such as ours, which has already defined its identity, generally stays for a limited time with that brand. There is only so much they can add to this identity before wanting to do something different. So the news that Susanne Deeken and Nicholas Knightly were leaving after nearly four years did not come as a surprise.

What was lovely about this slowly revolving door of talent was that no sooner had someone chosen to leave than someone equally talented would want to work with us. Such was the case with Amy Roberts. She simply appeared and was like a breath of fresh air. She had been working in Paris for several years with John Galliano on his own collections and on his work with Dior. I liked her instantly and she got on really well with Sophia, which made me happy, since Sophia had become incredibly important to me and to Ghost. She was doing all our beautiful embroideries, experimenting with new fabrics, and was my right hand with design and fit.

Hurricane Floyd and the bussed-in ladies had left me feeling bruised. Now felt like a good time to rejoin London Fashion Week, which had grown considerably in our absence, and we did our first show with Amy in February 2000. It was called 'Alice in Wonderland' and showed at teatime in the ballroom of the Dorchester Hotel in Park Lane. Inspiration came from the 19th-century portrait photographer Julia Margaret Cameron, and the opening music was 'The Woods', taken from Chick Corea's album *The Mad Hatter*, setting the scene of Alice in the enchanted woodland. The models all had long hair, and there were lots of bows on short dresses as well as our signature bias sheaths. As it was a tea party, we served little sandwiches, cakes and tea. At the end, Amy and I came out together.

The new generation of English models, Lily Cole, Rosie Huntington-Whiteley and Lizzy Jagger, had a magical presence that added to the show's surreal theme. It was a delightful show with Amy's inspired dreamy look, but the press by and large chose to ignore us, especially the trade press, with whom I became increasingly irritated. Ghost was a British success story. We had shown in New York in order to build an international business, from which the UK had benefited. Didn't we deserve at least a mention?

I didn't understand why we weren't included in the trade press round-up of shows. I never did find out. I wrote several angry letters, which thankfully I never sent.

My business decisions were generally sound, but not always. One of the most foolish decisions I ever made was to open a shop in Paris. We had already experienced French bureaucracy when, several years previously, we had booked, along with other designers, to do a trade show on a very large houseboat on the river Seine. Despite having done this show twice before on the same boat, on this occasion, for reasons we never fully understood, we were forcibly closed down. The organizers probably hadn't obtained the necessary permissions and permits in time. There ensued a mad rush to the new venue, the Saint James Albany Hotel on the Rue de Rivoli. Space there for the clothing rails was limited, so it was dog eat dog, but fortunately our American agent, Karen, had heard the news and got there before us. I arrived with the collection and my sales team to find her lying on the floor, arms and legs at full stretch, trying to keep us a space. It was a heroic effort, but unfortunately Karen was barely five feet tall.

Knowing how complex French bureaucracy could be and how unsuccessful various British businesses had been in France, I couldn't have been thinking straight when I took the decision to go ahead with our shop. But on the other hand, a Ghost store in Paris sounded so good, and the location, in the Rue du Jour near Les Halles, opposite Agnès B, a popular French mid-market fashion shop, seemed perfect.

The building we rented was old and had not been modernized, so the first necessity was a functioning toilet. Ted installed an electric one in the basement. Over the next few weeks, we poured money into making it a stylish, feminine, friendly place to try on and buy Ghost clothes.

No sooner had we finished the agreed work and opened the shop, in June 2000, than French bureaucracy struck. It seemed the front door wasn't wide enough for disabled access. It was useless pointing out that our door was exactly the same width as all the other doors in the street, including that of Agnès B across the road. It seemed there was one rule for French shop owners and another for non-French. We widened the door. Next we were fined for not having our sale during the officially designated French sale time. It didn't make any business sense to me that our shop had to put on a sale when we were told to rather than when it worked for us.

In addition, the taxes and obligations we were required to meet were a nightmare. If an employee's salary was £50,000 a year, they had to pay half of that to the government and the employer had to pay the same amount to the government. All of which meant that for the employee to take home £25,000, it cost the employer £75,000, with the lucky French state getting £50,000. On top of this, the employer had to continue paying wages if the business closed or the employee was made redundant or sacked. I wondered if the tax system in France explained why there were so many small family-run businesses, and why so many French people chose to work in countries outside France.

To add to our woes, the French staff we employed behaved in a similar way to the staff in LA. They were haughty and unfriendly to shoppers unless they were known or famous. In the end, it was all too much, and we closed after a year. Under French law at that time, we had to find alternative employment for the staff or continue to pay them and, of course, the government. We wrote to every fashion house to find jobs for them, but there was only one response, from Versace.

Disillusioned and frustrated after we closed the shop for the last time, Ris and I went to the Gare du Nord to catch the train back to London. As I stood outside the station, there was one final indignity – a pigeon shat on my head. It was hard not to take it personally.

While this complex employment and tax drama in Paris had been unfolding, we had another project in development: the production of a Ghost perfume. One of the top executives of international beauty products company Wella had seen our

Los Angeles shop and thought Ghost would be a great name for a perfume.

They approached us and I became excited. The idea of a perfume interested me far more than eyewear or hosiery. Wella, a German company that owned the French perfume company Rochas, initially asked me to work with an English company to develop the scent. This didn't work – the samples were completely wrong – so Wella put two of their most talented perfumers, Franzrudolf Lehnert and Michael Förster, in charge of the project.

Miracle of miracles, I liked and respected them both. They listened to me and my ideas, and although I knew little about their craft, I was very clear about what I wanted. Just as my clothes allowed women to express their individuality without the clothes overpowering them, I wanted the perfume to be subtle and feminine, not the kind that choked one in a small, enclosed place like a lift. I asked for aromas of jasmine and vanilla. When I found a beautiful cut-glass vase by Venini in the form of the body of a woman, I bought it and gave it to Franz as an inspiration to develop the bottle. Naturally it was too expensive to copy the Venini closely – it had too many curves – but in the end, Franz designed a distinctive and elegant bottle that gently curved in towards the middle.

Franz and Michael understood why I didn't like the English

trial samples and agreed to send the specifications to Grasse in the south of France, famous for its perfume industry. When the samples came back, the three of us would sit round a table in Ghost HQ with a bowl of coffee beans in the centre. I would be handed a long white strip to dip into the first sample and sniff. The same sample would be passed to Michael and then Franz. After each sample, the coffee beans were passed round to clear our noses, allowing us to move on to the next sample. I loved these perfume meetings. It was something different and I was using one of my senses in a way I had never used it before. It turned out that I had a talent for this, known as a good nose.

Ghost the Fragrance came out in September 2000, and it was everything I had wanted. Thousands of fragrances are released every year, but most do not survive more than one season, so it is a great source of pride to me that our original Ghost perfume is still popular today, more than 20 years on, and is available in many retail outlets including airports.

It was helped by a great advertising campaign, paid for by Wella and directed by Alister Mackie and me. We were given free rein, which was exciting. We wanted a strong face, rather than a pretty one, and we chose an unconventionally beautiful model called Colette. To shoot the ad we hired the virtually unknown photographers Mert Alas and Marcus Piggott, who went on to be two of the most famous photographers in their field. I wanted Colette to be seen rising out of the mist at sunrise. Mert and Marcus produced some ready-made background images for this, but I turned them down. I wanted the real thing and took the team down to my little house in Ramsgate, where the sun rose above the sea. The final shot was taken at around 5.30 am, which is why it is such a beautiful image, and I like to think that perhaps it helped to propel Mert and Marcus on their way to stardom.

We went on to produce five fragrances in all. For our second, I wanted the complete opposite of our first. This time I wanted a dark, chocolatey, sexy night-time perfume. I asked Franz to design a bottle in the shape of a half-moon. It was called Deep Night and it has been as successful as our first perfume, still on sale all these years later. We stayed with Mert and Marcus for the advertising campaign, which we shot with supermodel Liberty Ross. Both campaigns have been listed among the best 50 perfume advertisements ever made.

Liberty Ross later became Claudia's sister-in-law, when Claudia married Liberty's brother Atticus. He and Claudia had met in the world of music. Although Atticus had studied art, he also played the guitar, and the two of them put together a band called 12 Rounds.

My favourite of the five fragrances we produced was called Summer Breeze. I was invited to the home of Rochas in Paris to sample this fragrance. That was a very special pleasure for me, since my mother always wore Femme, a perfume by Rochas. How she would have loved to have visited the very elegant and luxurious home of her favourite perfume. Summer Breeze was in the same bottle as the original Ghost and was an interim fragrance only available for a short time. Its scent conjured up all the joys of summer.

The fourth fragrance came much later. It was called Serenity and was a very light perfume and the least popular of all the fragrances, partly because it was in a short, round bottle with none of the suggestiveness of our previous bottles. I'm not sure why we did that, because according to Michael and Franz, tall, thin bottles always sold better than short ones.

The last perfume we did was for men and was called Ghost Man. It was a great fragrance in a tall, rectangular bottle, and would have done really well, judging by the emails I have had over the years asking for it, but soon after its release, Wella was bought by Procter & Gamble, and with all the changes in marketing, press and sales teams, Ghost Man was forgotten.

After Wella was sold, Michael and Franz disappeared. The brilliant team we had created was gone. I tried collaborating with Procter & Gamble, but it didn't work. They came to me with their own storyboards and had no interest in any of my ideas, but as they owned the licence, I had no choice but to let them get on with it. However, to the best of my knowledge, they never produced a perfume with any staying power, and eventually sold the Ghost licence to a British company, Shaneel Enterprises. I really enjoyed my sortie into the world of perfume, but as I watched talented people being replaced by corporate entities, I knew that particular journey was over.

We did make some money from the perfume licence. Not a fortune, but enough for Ris to embark on an advertising campaign for Ghost. This was all very well, but advertising is an expensive business. It requires a model and a photographer with his crew, and then a minimum of a stylist, a make-up artist and a hairdresser, not to mention the cost of a studio and placing the finished advertisement in various magazines.

I was trying to work one day when Ris asked me to sign a cheque for £17,000. I asked him what it was for, and he told me it was to format the photograph for the different magazines in which we were placing advertisements. I suddenly had this image of me as a penniless old lady leafing through yellowing prints of our advertising campaigns. I refused to sign the cheque and told Ris that no more money was to be spent on advertising. Instead we would put it into the company pension fund, which would benefit us in the future far more than a few glossy pictures.

Ghost perfume advert with photograph by Mert Alas & Marcus Piggott.

Chapter Fourteen

Pressure

———

In September 2000, the same month that our first perfume was launched, we finally won a design award. During London Fashion Week, the Elle Style Awards were held. A glitzy affair hosted by Graham Norton and packed with fashion-world celebrities. Ghost won the Most Stylish Designer Award, which was presented to me by singer Marianne Faithfull.

As I stood talking to Marianne after the ceremony, a gushing young man pushed himself between us to tell her how well she had presented the award. Before she could reply, I turned to him and said, 'I think I collected the award rather well, don't you?'

Back at Ghost HQ afterwards, the staff were thrilled, and the award took pride of place.

I was at the helm of a global and commercially successful business that was growing at an extraordinary rate. But the demands were beginning to take a toll. I had always out-worked and out-partied people half my age and been proud of my energy and drive. I slept for about four hours at most each night and functioned on a cocktail of alcohol, drugs and sheer determination. How long could I keep it up?

The pressures on me were mounting. I loved creating clothes, but I did not enjoy the accessories, which involved a huge amount of additional work. We licensed eyewear and hosiery, but this still required input from me in much the same way as the perfume had. I found a shoe production designer, then I searched for shoes I liked that would complement our look and that the Ghost-buying public would want. Scarves were straightforward and we made them ourselves, but bags were much more difficult and involved another production designer, although Sophia designed and made a few with our fabrics. Nicholas Knightly designed the most gorgeous cushions and quilts for us before he left, and these were doing well. But it all seemed endless.

To add to my various stresses, a Japanese client wanting to spend over half a million pounds a year on Ghost refused to speak to me because I was a woman. I had to hand him over to Ris, which left me fuming.

On top of all this, my father's health was deteriorating, and he expected me to help him. Now in his eighties and still determined to carry on working, he would call me to his flat to take dictation that rarely made any sense. I recently found a letter he had dictated in an old book. It was addressed to the Honourable Alla Adgedy, and read, 'please ask for Tacchi, can't make a proposal because Ping Pong team have to do specifications with independent advisers for parliament work would be done by associated firm Marconi'. I had to try and make sense of these dictations and find the things he had misplaced, such as his chequebook, in one of the most disorganized offices imaginable. He had a secretary during office hours, and a live-in girlfriend, but he told me he didn't trust either of them. I had been a good daughter since my mother died and had gone to his flat for dinner once a week without fail. These had mostly been pleasant occasions until now, when he seemed determined to drive me into a spiral of intolerance, impatience and exhaustion. As far as I knew, he didn't have dementia, although he was never tested, but he definitely had a very bad temper. He would regularly come into the office, storm into whatever meeting I was in and start shouting at me in front of staff. Half the time I had no idea what he was on about; it would be 'Where's that green chair I left at your house, have you got rid of it?' Or 'I can't find my notes.' Or 'You didn't deal with Tacchi like I asked you.'

I would steer him firmly out of the room and tell him I'd be over later to sort out whatever it was. He certainly expected to take priority over anything else I was doing. I believe he was proud of my success but also a little jealous that I had been able to achieve something on my own. He had guaranteed my overdraft at the beginning of Ghost, but other than that I had not needed him, and maybe this wounded his ego.

Meanwhile, in New York, our agents were becoming complacent, so Ris and I flew over to see what was going on. What had been the Ghost showroom, where our collections had been on display to be shown to buyers, had now become the hang-out and eating room for the staff. We decided it was time to open our own office, showroom and shop.

We found the perfect place for an English shop in Bond Street. This was in Lower Manhattan, also known as Downtown, and was a road that ran off Broadway in an area officially called the Bowery – ironic, since Michael's New York film back in 1972 was to have been about drunks in the Bowery. The area was totally downbeat then, but by 2000 it was getting better, and the premises were perfect for us. There was a basement big enough to accommodate an office, showroom and stockroom, while upstairs, at ground level, was the glass-fronted retail area, which had formerly been used as a meeting place for the Muslim Brotherhood. There were a couple of other fashion businesses in Bond Street, and one restaurant,

Me and Andrew at the top of the Twin Towers, 1994.

The New York store.

but other than that it was still fairly run-down, and many of the buildings in the street housed artists on controlled rents.

After securing the tenancy, Ris and I returned to London, leaving it to Ted to work his magic and turn the premises into another fantastic Ghost store.

While I had been busy with perfume and a multitude of accessories, Ris was building up our concessions. We now had 15: Harrods and Liberty in London; Selfridges in London, Birmingham and Manchester; Harvey Nichols in London and Leeds; House of Fraser in Kensington, Oxford Street, Guildford, Bluewater and Glasgow. We also had one in Printemps in Paris, one in Denmark and another in Dublin.

By this time, I had given Ris 20 per cent of the company. He had earned it; he ran the whole business side of the operation and was endlessly hard-working, very clever and totally loyal. He was much more than just financial director; he was part of Ghost and we were very close. I had gifted him 10 per cent on one of his birthdays, and another 10 per cent later on. We both wanted the same thing, the success of the company, and I trusted him implicitly. While I tended to be more comfortable with selling to shops wholesale, Ris knew that retail was where the greater profits lay, and I was happy to let him get on with building up the concessions.

Ghost's employees now numbered a hundred, with the shop

and concession staff making up a good proportion of this. At Ghost HQ, lunch was still cooked every day, and annual outings to Ramsgate continued but, perhaps inevitably, we didn't have quite the same family atmosphere we had once enjoyed. While the number of staff played a part in this, much of the reason lay in my increasingly erratic behaviour. I would shout at people, which I had never done before, and my staff, who had always seen me as totally approachable, started to steer clear of me.

Adjacent to our offices was a partially cleared plot of land that had previously been a marble works. In the middle of this was a small office. The entire site was for sale, and since we were running out of space, Ris and I decided to use some of the pension fund money to buy the site, with the intention of building a new design studio.

In the meantime, I started to use the small office as my personal workspace, which turned out to be disastrous. Instead of being in the middle of things, where I could see and hear exactly what was going on and monitor everything from finance to design and production, I was hiding away from the endless decisions I was asked to make.

As my isolation grew, my dependence on alcohol and cocaine grew with it. I no longer had to hide my drug use or drinking, as I had complete privacy. I would go in and out of the Ghost building when necessary, but would stay late into the evening in the little office, pretending to work while drinking organic red wine and using cocaine. I wrote irrational letters that I never sent and, worse still, I would see how many words I could make out of someone's name. If I couldn't make at least ten words, I would dismiss that person in my mind. I was in trouble, and yet I always thought I could stop. Even at this late stage, it never occurred to me that I might be an alcoholic or an addict. If I was still functioning, going to fittings, correcting line sheets and doing my work, then surely I had everything under control?

Andrew and I were seeing less and less of each other, if only because we were working to two very different timescales. In addition to his drumming career, he had started to make his presence felt on national radio, working with the team on BBC Radio 1 writing sketches and jokes. As his new direction gathered pace, our domestic arrangements changed. He would be out of the house by 5.30 in the morning and go to bed at 9.30 pm. I would come home late and then be asleep when he left for work. Occasionally he would be getting up while I was still entertaining people I'd brought home for a drink.

He took to sleeping in the studio on the ground floor, at the back of the house, so that I didn't wake him when I came back late or with friends. He was always patient, but as time passed, he was clearly becoming unhappy with the arrangement, concerned about my isolation during the day and my absence from home in the evenings. For my part, I just wanted to be left alone. At this point I probably should have asked for help, but it wasn't in me, so I convinced myself that I didn't have a problem and carried on.

Two days before the grand opening in New York, my friend Mandy and I flew over and moved into a rented apartment, where we proceeded to get off our heads on drink and drugs. We were both asleep when the shop opened, and we only came to our blurry senses when Andrew appeared.

We managed to get ourselves together somehow, and to stagger down to the shop, where, despite the fact that they were already halfway through proceedings, we were greeted with cheers, and only a few scowls. The shop looked great and was full of people, most of whom I didn't know, so I smiled dutifully at everyone and shook the hands that were held out to me.

Fortunately we'd decided to open with cocktails rather than a full party, so I only had to manage an hour of socializing before I could go back to the flat with Andrew. I was apologetic and headed straight for bed.

If I thought I had got away with it, I was wrong. On my return to London, I received a letter from Ris, saying my behaviour was unacceptable. I was shocked and upset, and promised him I would get myself together. Andrew was also beside himself, concerned that I was heading for a total breakdown. He said that if I didn't agree to do something about it, he didn't know if he could continue living with me.

Somewhere deep inside my addled brain, I was beginning to accept that maybe Andrew and Ris weren't making it up. Maybe there was something wrong with me. I didn't want to upset the people around me, and I definitely didn't want to lose Andrew, who I loved, so I decided to call my daughter in Los Angeles, who understood these things and had said to me on the last few occasions we had seen each other, 'Mum, please look after yourself.'

Claudia had been touring America with 12 Rounds. She and Atticus had decided to stay in LA and make a life for themselves there. They were in the process of buying a house in the Hollywood Hills and were about to embark on an incredibly successful career composing the music for commercials and, more importantly, films. Later Atticus would join Trent Reznor's industrial rock band Nine Inch Nails, and together they went on to win two Oscars, a clutch of Grammys and an Emmy for their work on music soundtracks.

I asked Claudia if she could research somewhere for me to get better, a cure-all place. By this time Andrew had left the Radio 1 breakfast show and joined Radio 4, where he wrote a critically acclaimed sci-fi comedy called *The Routemasters*, which starred Amanda Donohoe as a time-travelling art thief. He followed this with a musical written with his friend Nick Romero and starring comedian Bob Monkhouse and musician Suggs. After this he decided to take some time off, and enrolled at UCLA for an intensive series of courses on comedy improv, sitcom and film scriptwriting. If I was going to deal with my problem and get better, it made sense to me to do it in Los Angeles when Andrew would be there, and where I would be close to my daughter.

Claudia found a place high in the hills above Malibu, which was expensive but at least fairly exclusive, since maximum capacity was 15 students, as they liked to call their inmates. I agreed to check it out on my next trip to LA, but said I wasn't quite ready. I reasoned that there was another collection to design and sell and another show to do. How could I possibly hide myself away?

In the meantime, I agreed to try to moderate my drinking and improve my behaviour. I promised not to shout at anyone and to be patient, polite and calm, though it seems I wasn't very good at it. But for the moment, anyway, life carried on, and Ghost carried on designing, opening concessions, and showing during London Fashion Week. I believe I moderated my using a fraction, since I managed all my work and welcomed the press at our shows with broad smiles. I also threw a big party for Andrew on his fortieth birthday, in March 2001. I was fine. Why did I need help?

It was September 2001, and our next show was approaching. By this time, New York, once last on the fashion calendar, was first, and New York Fashion Week had just finished when news came that shocked and stunned the world. Two passenger planes hijacked by al-Qaeda, Islamic terrorists, had flown into the Twin Towers of the World Trade Center. Thousands of people had died or were injured, and in the chaos and debris of the aftermath it would be a long time before they could discover just how many.

New York was in shock. Models phoned me in tears to tell me they couldn't get to the UK in time for our show, since the airports were closed. I didn't know what to do. Should we cancel? In the end, I ordered a truckload of flowers and greenery with which we lined both sides of the runway. For the finale of the show we made a long white dress with layers and layers of organza from the waist down so that it had huge volume. On the lower layers we hand-embroidered the words Love and Peace in yellow, blue and white. It was a sad show, and for the first time in Ghost's history, there was no post-show party.

Chapter Fifteen

Detox

———

Mutterings from my family and Andrew started up again. What was I going to do about my problem? The more they went on at me, the more I isolated myself in my little hideout, continuing to write letters I never sent and play with people's names. Had I known about Sudoku then, I probably would have played that all night.

If I had sent the letters, I would have made more enemies than I already had and got myself into a lot of trouble. I recently found some of these outpourings in an old notebook; they illustrate my state of mind at the time.

One of my favourite targets was *Drapers*:

Dear Editor,

Ghost was ignored for the second consecutive season by *Drapers* in their round-up reviews of the shows. Unlike most of the designers *Drapers* chose to review, Ghost has a business. It supports many families in many parts of England since our manufacturing is entirely UK based and supplies over 100 independent retailers throughout the UK. I believe all the above subscribe to your magazine. It would be nice to have some support from our trade press. It would be even better if this trade press could grow up, see what's in their own front garden and stop fixating on unproven newcomers, most of whom mean nothing to *Drapers* readers now or in the future. One of the 'New Stars' reviewed had a dress recently in one of the Sunday papers retailing at £9,000, hardly relevant to people who work their arses off in a thankless business.

I have found several versions of this and other letters. I was very obviously not in a good state as I sat there, downing red wine and cocaine and fuming.

Here are some lines from another one I wrote to one of the dailies:

Dear Sir,

Rarely have I read such pretentious negative rubbish as your reporter's recent article.

If your reporter wants to write poetry or philosophize then give her a column for that purpose, but please . . . don't let her near fashion. She not only has a total lack of understanding of the fashion industry, but cheerfully plays with the lives of thousands of people with complete and utter irresponsibility. She should consider her country, its international status, and the individuals who by dedication, hard work and self-sacrifice try to keep British fashion alive. I for one will not break my back, stick my neck out, and incur near-total stress having a fashion show for the sake of British fashion while the likes of your reporter are allowed to run around destroying what is left of the UK's credibility in the fashion industry and wrecking thousands of lives in the process.

I knew I couldn't go on in this way. I could hear an inner voice telling me that maybe, just maybe, I needed help. The paranoia I was beginning to experience confirmed this. I became angry at the smallest things, terrified that it was all going to be taken away from me and shouting, often without provocation, at the people I loved.

Prompted by my family, I agreed to get in touch with the smart place that Claudia had researched, although privately I wasn't about to commit to anything more than a phone call. I spoke to Teresa, who was in charge there, and who I decided to refer to as Mother Teresa, as she sounded so spiritual and caring. She suggested I pay them a visit on my next trip to LA, and I agreed, while making it clear that I was just coming to have a look.

Before I could travel, though, there was another show to do in London. For every show we produced a programme, with numbered looks on the inside, credits on the last page and a piece at the beginning on the inspiration for the show. The talented fashion journalists Susannah Frankel and Iain R. Webb contributed most of these inspiration pieces, but for some reason I composed the introduction for this show, and it's a relief to know that I was capable of writing something positive in the fog of addiction: 'The feel and sensibility of this collection is taken from the gutters of Victoriana . . . not the well-heeled. Floozies flounce, magpies flutter, urchins pick pockets. Mixed with this is an element of the Wild West. The brave women pioneers and the saloon hussies.'

The models began the show in knickerbockers teamed with lace-panelled high-necked blouses, and the final section was over-the-top evening wear. It was a good show, and afterwards we had another mad party with the McQueen team at a local restaurant/bar that we took over for the night. Everyone got very drunk. Alexander McQueen made a brief entrance, but it was too noisy and chaotic even for him and he left.

After the show and the party, I got on a flight to LA. I had arranged to visit what I thought of as the cure-all place, actually an upmarket rehabilitation centre in Malibu, where Claudia and I had lived when she was born.

My visit had been arranged with someone called Diana, who told me that Teresa would be available to show me round. But when I arrived at the centre, a large house high up in the Malibu Hills, I was told that Teresa was busy with a group. I had to wait for nearly an hour before she appeared, and I wasn't happy, although I managed to keep my temper in check. She showed me round the house, which had beautiful views looking out over the Pacific, grounds big enough to go for walks, and a small swimming pool, and explained that the meals were all cooked in-house by an accredited chef. Not so bad, I thought. Maybe it would do me good to have a month's rest here.

After the visit, I stayed in LA for another few days to spend time with Claudia, and then returned to London. I hadn't yet booked into the rehab centre and I kept finding ridiculous excuses not to. I was still not convinced I was an alcoholic or an addict, even though this denial was flatly contradicted by my terror at the thought of giving up my two best friends, wine and cocaine.

I was still writing angry letters, and thankfully still not sending them. I fired this one off to the hapless Diana, who had booked my visit to the Malibu centre.

Dear Diana,

I am beginning to wonder who needs help most, you or me!

You arranged for me to meet Teresa on Tuesday March 11th at 11.30. Not only did you forget to inform her of this meeting, you should also have been aware (I presume you know your schedule) that she would be busy with a group at this time . . . For someone in charge of admissions you are doing a good job of putting me off. I believe my behaviour to be honest and courteous. I expect your behaviour to be the same.

At the beginning of April, Andrew left me to start his writing courses at UCLA. Perhaps his absence was the final prompt I needed, because soon after he left, I thought, what the hell, it won't do me any harm, maybe I should go.

I used up my Virgin air miles on a flight to Los Angeles, where, after spending a week with Andrew, I packed a bag and headed off into the hills above Malibu. I was nervous and unsure, ready to turn tail and run if it all got too much. And I almost fell at the first hurdle, when to my horror I had to share a room with another woman, since the place was full to capacity. She was a wealthy young woman who spent her time reading gossip magazines with a plastic guard over her teeth to whiten them. Conversation between us was nil.

That first week was a nightmare. Mentally I felt like a ghost, which I suppose was apt. I was an empty shell; I'd lost all sense of who or what I was.

Withdrawal was awful; it made my hands swell up and itch constantly. I had terrible nightmares and was often in floods of tears. The various pills I was given for the first three days to ease the symptoms only helped fractionally. I had held it together for so long; now that the props I'd relied on had been taken away, I was in meltdown.

I had no intention of killing myself, but because I couldn't stop crying, I was put on suicide watch, which meant I was constantly followed.

After the first week, however, life began to improve. I was given a room to myself, the withdrawal pangs subsided, and I met some interesting companions among the other residents. There were two musicians from well-known bands, a very famous female singer, an actor or two, and the odd heir and heiress to well-known international corporations. One of them was convinced the coyotes that howled at night were calling him. We had to forcibly restrain him from going out to join them. A famous actor escaped one night to meet a friend waiting outside with alcohol and drugs. I don't know how he got past the locked gates, but he did. He made his way back to the centre before the next morning, but he must have been completely wasted, because he ended up in the wrong house, and a startled young woman found him passed out in her bed.

Stories like this provided much-needed entertainment, because our days were filled with lectures and meetings intended to help us change our ways. We had many discussions on how we felt, which I found hard, since I didn't know how to put into words my bewilderment and alienation. I was lost in a strange place with people I didn't know and who didn't know me.

What I did enjoy was the art therapy, and learning how to communicate with horses at a nearby stable. We were shown how to walk with a horse while talking to it, and it was a memorable experience.

From time to time a helicopter from *The Hollywood Reporter* flew over attempting to spy on us and get some gossip. I knew I was unlikely to interest them, so I didn't worry.

As time passed, I felt the faint beginnings of a sense of freedom. It was a feeling I hadn't experienced for many years, and a desire in me to find myself began to grow. I was a good student, I followed all the suggestions offered to help me through each day, even getting down on my knees every morning to pray to a God or higher power that I didn't understand or believe in. I rationalized this by accepting that I was powerless over virtually everything. I have since come to believe that for me, God or the higher power referred to is present in everything that exists, and I recently learned that this makes me a pantheist.

My time in rehab was life-changing and I felt very privileged to have gone to such an excellent place. At first it was the small things I noticed, like feeling healthier and more alert, but then I felt the bigger changes happening in me: a sense of freedom and well-being alongside profound vulnerability and lack of confidence, and the fear of relapse should I find myself isolated or under pressure.

I responded so well that I was allowed, along with one of the male residents, to spend the last week of the four-week course at the centre's beach house, unsupervised. Being in the house reminded me of my early married days, when I would stare at the rolling waves of the Pacific from my bedroom window. I loved that, and I would walk on the beach whenever I could.

A staff member lived in the house, and he would drive the two of us every morning up the steep hills to the centre, so that we could take part in the day's activities, before bringing us back in the evening.

After the first week, we were allowed visitors on Saturdays, and Claudia and Andrew always came to see how I was getting on. Atticus came too, at least once. I was so happy to see them and to be reminded of the outside world.

After two weeks in rehab, I decided to phone my father, worried about how he would be managing without me. I hadn't told him I was going away, but I was sure he must have missed my visits. He picked up the phone and talked at me for 20 minutes about himself, never asking how I was or where I was, and then said goodbye. I didn't even have the chance to tell him that his grandson was getting married very soon. I wasn't really surprised. A little hurt, maybe, but I was used to his slight narcissism, and I shrugged it off.

Before leaving rehab, we had to write an exit plan on how we were going to live. I wrote, very proudly, that I was going to get seven hours' sleep every night. Mother Teresa told me it wasn't enough. I had to get eight hours. Fat chance, I thought. I'd been surviving on about four hours a night for months, if not years, so the idea of eight felt like untold luxury, not to mention virtually unattainable.

On our last day, we had a completion ceremony, when each of us was given a gold coin. On either side was a phrase that indicated our progress and likely chance of success in maintaining sobriety. One side of my coin read 'Reach for the stars' and the other side 'Live each day to the full', which seemed like a pretty good outcome. I was proud of myself.

I was gratified to see that my arch-enemy, the wife of a famous sportsman who had insisted on hogging the television for every baseball match she could find, and was generally obnoxious, had 'Stumbling blocks' written on one side of her coin. I never discovered what was on the other side, but I felt very smug.

After the ceremony, I was released back into the real world. At first I felt very uncomfortable; everything felt strange and unfamiliar. I was frail and vulnerable, shy and unsure of myself. The barrier I had put up to shield me from the world had gone, and it would take me time to regain my confidence and get used to the new me. I couldn't imagine how someone who has been locked up in prison must feel after their release, if this was how I was feeling after just one month in an exclusive rehab.

Andrew was in LA for another month, so I stayed with him for a few days before returning to England. I had been away from work for weeks, plus William and Samantha were due to marry in a couple of weeks. I was incredibly happy for them; they were clearly so right for each other. They had met at Latimer Place, the restaurant William and Albert had opened. While the restaurant didn't last more than three years, their relationship did, and Samantha had gone on to work on the creative side of advertising at Saatchi & Saatchi.

Claudia flew with me back to England, and I was grateful for her support. I wasn't yet ready to face everything on my own.

I arrived back at work to a shock. My very private little office in the middle of the old marble works had been bulldozed. At the time, Ris told me it was because he wanted to get on with building the new design studio; it was only years later that he admitted that the real reason was to prevent me from isolating again. I was furious, and immediately rented a small office nearby. I didn't feel up to working in a noisy, chaotic building full of people frequently suffering with hangovers. I worked from this little office for three months before returning full-time to the hub of Ghost.

Meanwhile, William and Samantha's wedding was imminent, and everything appeared to be in a state of total chaos. They had decided to get married on the beach in Ramsgate, which sounded charming but was utterly impractical. It was useless trying to tell them that they could not have a legal marriage there, and what if the tide was in and there *was* no beach? Besides, they had already sent out the invitations. They decided they would have the beach wedding and then legalize their marriage at some point in a register office.

So we all headed off to Ramsgate, where Claudia and I booked a hotel room in nearby Broadstairs. The catering and preparation was to be done in my cottage, and we knew there would be a lot of partying, endless noise, and drunken wedding guests crashing out on the sofas and in the bedrooms, which was not what I needed when I was less than three weeks out of rehab.

Two houses up the road from the cottage was a forlorn, dilapidated building where busloads of old folk on day trips to the seaside had once come to eat fish and chips. William had got permission to use it for the wedding reception, but it was in urgent need of deep cleaning.

Claudia and I set about trying to make it presentable. We swept and washed the floors, bought candles to put on the tables, and generally did everything we could to make it more wedding-friendly.

On the day, it was pouring with rain, which was heartbreaking – the one thing no one could do anything about. The ceremony was quickly transferred to the fish and chip building where the lunch was to be held, but that didn't save the guests' wedding outfits from being soaked and their hats ruined.

As the chefs William had hired were preparing the lunch at the cottage, the smoke alarms went off. The alarm company called the mobile number of the first keyholder, Andrew, who was five thousand miles away in Los Angeles. He was woken at three in the morning and tried desperately to get his head around why he was being asked to check if there was a fire in Ramsgate.

Naturally lunch was very late, and while everyone waited for the food, I tried to be hospitable and talk to people, but it wasn't easy, since voices all around me were getting louder and louder as copious amounts of alcohol were consumed.

Food did eventually arrive, at which point I couldn't find a chair to sit on. They had all been taken. Claudia took one look at me and realized I was getting overwhelmed. She grabbed my arm and took me to the car, and we went back to our hotel. It had been the first test of my sobriety, and it was a big one. I did find the strength to resist, but the chaos around me was too much. I knew William would understand.

He and Samantha had secretly married legally the morning before the chaos began, and much to my huge delight, they are still in a wonderfully happy marriage. They now have three lovely children, Saul, who as I write has just turned 19, Isiah, who is 15, and Azura, who is 11.

Fern Mallis (then Executive Director of the Council of Fashion Designers of America) and me.

Chapter Sixteen

Change

Back at work, I found it difficult to concentrate for any length of time. For the first six weeks, every morning at around 11 am I would leave work and go to Coffee Bean on Portobello Road, where I would have a large, very strong coffee and a chocolate muffin. Needless to say, I expanded.

I no longer had quite the energy and enthusiasm I had always been known for. My confidence and bravado had gone along with the drugs and alcohol. One or two of my staff were not happy with my new sober self, and one of them deliberately left a piece of hashish on the passenger seat of my car. I don't know if the culprit intended to test me or tempt me. I am sorry to say I gave in to temptation. I also had a glass of red wine in a restaurant. My French grandmother had told me, 'One must drink a glass of wine after a meal. It is necessary for the digestive system.' Her words were still ringing in my head.

However, neither the wine nor the hashish sat well with my conscience or with my digestive system. I became extremely depressed and couldn't stop crying.

Two lovely ladies found me in this state outside an Alcoholics Anonymous meeting and gently led me inside. I didn't use or drink again after that meeting, and it is now close on 20 years since I have had a drug or a drink. I found the strength to go to meetings regularly, to pray every day, despite not knowing who or what I was praying to, and I found a sponsor to take me through the Twelve Steps. The steps are amazing, and I am convinced that if everyone did steps four to twelve, the world would be a much better place. Instead of war there would be love. Everyone would be much kinder to their fellow citizens, and honesty, tolerance and open-mindedness would prevail.

AA and NA (Narcotics Anonymous) meetings became all-important for me. I needed the support of people in these meetings in order to maintain my sobriety and stay clean. It took me a long time to find my true self and to feel I was standing on solid ground again, but bit by bit I dealt with the past and put it behind me. I made amends to everyone I had hurt, except for my former husband, Michael. It took me a long time to understand how my divorcing him had hurt him. For years I had only been aware of what he had put me through. But eventually I did see his perspective too, and I am now on good terms with him. I can't live in the past, only in the present. I still go to meetings and try to help newcomers. I have also made many good friends over the years who I can turn to at any time if I need to.

Back in early 2002, Ghost needed me, and I tried to throw myself back into it. The previous few years had been an extraordinary whirlwind of a journey, for the business and for me, and I needed to take stock and see where we were. Unbelievably, given my level of distraction, Ghost was still going well, thanks to the dedication of my staff, especially Ris. But the fashion world had altered dramatically since the eighties and nineties, and I needed to understand how it had changed and what we needed to do.

Fashion shows, which had been 30 minutes long, now ran for only 10 to 15 minutes. More importantly, buying patterns were different. When I began Ghost, mums would still bring their daughters to London twice a year to dress them and themselves for the coming season. This was no longer the case. Women, young and old, now bought when the mood took them, or when they needed something. And the choices they were offered had increased vastly. In the eighties, there were few designers. By the year 2000, there were hundreds. There were so many brands that retailers no longer knew exactly what to buy or what their customers wanted, so rather than putting their trust in a few collections and ordering across their range, they hedged their bets by buying a little from lots of different brands. This meant that instead of a few large orders, we had dozens of smaller ones. And inevitably we could no longer get to know our buyers as we once had – there were so many of them.

The other problem was keeping our prices competitive. There were fewer and fewer designers manufacturing in the UK, because it was cheaper to manufacture in China, India, Eastern Europe and many other places in the world. As the 21st century began, our wholesale business was very slowly declining.

With a heavy heart, I asked our head of production to research alternative production outside the UK. I had worked with our small units, scattered around England, for many years. I had seen their children through their school years and watched them grow up, and I didn't want to have to close these units down and take the manufacturing abroad. So I didn't push my production people very hard, with the result that they did nothing.

Added to this, the wonderful dyers in Leicestershire that we had relied on for so long had shrunk from the 500 employees they'd had when we first went to them to a handful of staff. They hadn't modernized their factory, their system was outdated, water was heated miles away from the washing machines, and their top dyers had been poached by other countries.

Despite all this, I was not about to give up, but I knew that we were going to have to move with the times.

I hadn't changed my opinion of the British Fashion Council and the press, who I felt had ignored Ghost, so for our next show I decided on a different venue, rather than the tents outside the Natural History Museum where the shows had been moved to after Olympia. I opted for 33 Portland Place, a very large Regency house just off Regent Street, which was available to rent on a daily basis.

Sam Gainsbury, who had so brilliantly produced Alexander McQueen's shows, was a friend, and she had offered to help me if I needed it. I did need help, and she agreed to produce the show, which took place on several levels of the house and involved a lot of stair-walking. Perhaps because of the stairs, it was a good show but not spectacular. We followed it with a quiet party in Covent Garden. How parties had changed since my new-found sobriety!

After this show, I foolishly decided to return to New York, where we had been so successful. We hadn't shown there since our show had been moved in the Hurricane Floyd debacle of 1999. I should have known better. It is impossible to recreate what has been, and the fact that it was to be our thirteenth show in New York should have been a warning to me. The Gramercy Park Hotel was in the process of being refurbished by entrepreneur Ian Schrager and artist Julian Schnabel – it was to become an extremely arty, stylish and expensive hotel for the rich and famous – so we stayed in a less expensive hotel off Washington Square in Lower Manhattan. We showed in the tents in Bryant Park, and it was pretty much a non-event; we were old news, and there were lots of newcomers all trying to grab the spotlight. We didn't have the same supermodel cast and there was nothing revolutionary in our designs. Somehow the pizzazz of our earlier collections had gone, and we were just another brand.

We booked a bar for the after-show celebration. Everyone except me got drunk on apple martinis, and one of my team was so drunk he missed his flight home. Gatecrashers were still a problem and I hardly recognized anyone at this event, but my lovely Andrew made it his mission to try to throw them all out, which was very amusing.

Shortly after our show, Fern Mallis, Executive Director of the Council of Fashion Designers of America, got in touch with me. Fern had been credited with transforming New York Fashion Week into one of the big four events on the international fashion calendar. We weren't close friends, but we liked and respected each other. She told me she wanted to make Los Angeles the fifth international event on the calendar, and asked me if we would show in LA instead of New York the following season. She told me that Rick Owens, one of the better-known designers, had already agreed to show there, and she was looking for another big name. I was delighted. What could be better? We had a shop there where we could work, and I would be near my daughter, who could arrange accommodation for my team. It was new and different, and the thought of being the first fashion company to show in LA was exciting. I replied with an emphatic yes. My team were thrilled. A free trip to sunny LA, what could be better?

Los Angeles was to be the last stop in the fashion calendar and our show would be in April 2003. So in March, while London was in the midst of its fashion week, the Ghost team set off. We took Amy and Sophia, studio head Jill Entwistle, pattern cutters Ali and Neil, machinists Debbie and Francis, and Jenny, who had taken over our public relations from Alex, who had left to have a baby, plus Ris. Casting director Sidonie and I went a few days ahead of the rest, to start looking for our models.

The team stayed in hotels on Sunset Strip, not far from our shop, and since the space above the shop was empty, the Epsteins, who owned it, allowed us to use it to set up our sewing machines and all the paraphernalia necessary for preparing and fitting the clothes.

When Sidonie and I began casting for the show, it immediately became apparent that we had a problem. Show models were few and far between in LA; girls were there to show off their bodies rather than clothes. Some had enlarged breasts, and some had enlarged bottoms, neither of which worked for the runway. Fortunately, top model Kirsty Hume, who had modelled for us in New York, was now living in LA, and she agreed to be our star model. The theme of the show, since we were in Hollywood, was Disney. We employed a new stylist, Nick Cox and made little versions of Bambi, which were sewn onto the outfits. Claudia put together great show music for us, as she had done in the very early days.

The show was held in the official venue, downtown in the business district, and when we arrived, there were paparazzi everywhere. It seemed both the audience and the press thought they were coming to see something akin to the Oscars. Celebrities appeared, posing and smiling for the cameras, and one elderly gentleman – I have no idea who he was – walked in with a pretty blonde on his arm only to realize that all the photographers were busy with an actress. He promptly walked out again and made another entrance once they were paying attention. We had invited all our buyers in California, and a few of them came, but the rest of the audience were straight out of a film guide. There was no international fashion press, and unlike the shows we had done where the front rows were full of journalists, I only saw one person taking notes, a journalist from the *Los Angeles Times*.

The show was great fun and well received. The post-show party, arranged by our publicist, Marilyn Heston, was in the trendy Skybar of the Mondrian Hotel; the word 'Ghost' was illuminated in the centre of the pool. It was all very glamorous and lovely, but not to be repeated. The cost and effort were not worth the outcome; it didn't help our bank balance or result in any worthwhile press.

On the plus side, it had been extremely pleasant to spend time with my daughter, and it had also helped my recovery. Every morning at 7.30 am I had gone to an AA meeting in a big hall near our shop. The meetings were attended by well over 200 people, from actors and business executives to down-and-outs. The speaker would start by asking if there were any alcoholics present in the room, and everyone would cheer, put up their hand and shout, 'I am.' I enjoyed these meetings, and they strengthened my resolve to never drink again. But Los Angeles was never to become the fifth fixture on the international fashion calendar.

Back in London, it was becoming increasingly clear that we had to move our production out of the UK. Our prices were no longer as competitive as they had once been. This wasn't helped by the fact that the pound had slumped against the dollar, and the introduction of the euro in Europe wasn't helpful either. Added to this, there was mounting competition as more designers entered the industry and more companies copied Ghost. To continue manufacturing in the UK would be tantamount to suicide. I told our production manager to investigate Romania, where they were actively looking for work, and where it was much cheaper than the UK. And this time I meant what I said. It tore me apart, but it had to be done.

At the same time that we began manufacturing in the country of my father's birth, he was diagnosed with lung cancer. This was his second cancer diagnosis. A few years earlier, he had been told he had prostate cancer. He had held a big dinner party in a Greek restaurant to which he had invited his Iranian former girlfriend, his current live-in girlfriend and his family. At this dinner he had announced his imminent death. We had all broken plates, and his ex had danced on the table while his live-in girlfriend pretended to cry. He had gone on to live a normal life for the next seven years.

Now they had found a cancerous growth on his lung. He couldn't believe it, since he prided himself on having given up cigarettes and taken up cigars. He underwent surgery. I was by his side when he awoke from the operation and threw his mobile phone at the nurse. I apologized to her, but she informed me that old people coming round from an anaesthetic often behaved like this. I prayed that should I find myself in a similar situation one day, I would show a little more restraint.

After this operation, he was in and out of hospital over a long period. Two ladies from our new production team in Romania were visiting. I told them about my Romanian dad not being well, and they offered to visit him at his flat to cheer him up. He was so happy to speak Romanian with them, and he told them he would love to eat his favourite Romanian dish, *mămăligă*, a kind of porridge made from cornmeal, feta cheese, sour cream and milk. The two of them returned the following night and cooked it for him. Producing our clothes in Romania did have hidden benefits, but it didn't help the guilt and sadness I felt about the families in the UK who had lost their livelihoods when Ghost stopped manufacturing with them.

Soon after eating his favourite dish, Dad was hospitalized again. At this point his behaviour became even more impossible. I would arrive at work, and just as I was absorbed in something, the phone would go and he would croak, 'COME NOW!' and hang up. I would drop everything, rush to the hospital near Hammersmith, fight for a parking space, climb endless flights of stairs, and run through several corridors until I reached him. 'What is it, Daddy? What's the problem?' I would ask breathlessly.

'Phone, can't reach,' he would reply, pointing to his mobile phone, which was just out of reach.

There was no point asking him how he had managed to phone me at the office, or why he couldn't have asked one of the nurses to give him his phone. I felt proud of myself for not screaming at him, which I wouldn't have been able to do a couple of years earlier. I had learned in recovery that I couldn't change another person, only myself, and I was learning to be more patient, tolerant and forgiving. Before going to see him in hospital, I would generally say the serenity prayer I had learned, about accepting the things one cannot change, and then I would take a few deep breaths. Often, at his request, I would stay with him until he fell asleep. His girlfriend, who was nine years older than me, was unable to come since she had a bad leg and said she couldn't manage the long walk into the hospital.

One of the better memories I have of that time was of an old Indian man opposite my father. He would sit cross-legged on his bed, and every time he saw me he would say, 'You've got to be fit to be here, you know.' He was referring to the barely edible food and the fact that when a nurse was needed there was never one around. More often than not it was me who would help Dad get to the toilet.

It was all very well going to the hospital every day, but there was a collection to do, another show to put on, and Amy was very pregnant. The easiest solution was to show in the official venue, in the tents outside the Natural History Museum. We had a delightful show, and I was surprised and pleased to discover that the whole process was far more organized and efficient than before.

For this autumn 2002 show, our look was a combination of Empire line and ethnic embroidery designed by Sophia. We had finally solved the problem of preserving the colours of embroidery in the manufacturing process: polyester thread, unlike cotton, kept its colour when it was boiled and dyed, emerging a fraction faded but still clear. I was proud of this show, and at the end Amy and I came out together.

The post-show celebration was minimal, but soon after this we had a big baby shower for Amy, which in my opinion was much nicer than the riotous parties we were known for. I'm not sure some of my staff agreed. They hadn't got used to the new me, and I seemed to slightly dampen their spirits. I was quieter and more thoughtful, and sometimes not quite there. Why wasn't I shouting at them? they wondered. But they all knew I had been to rehab, and most of them respected the change in me, despite the fact that this inevitably subdued the atmosphere.

In November 2003, Amy gave birth to a son. She returned to work six weeks later with her baby, Max, in tow, to work on our next show. I was delighted to have Max join us. A baby was a lovely addition to our working lives, and we all enjoyed having him in the office.

By New Year 2004, I was tired. It had been an exhausting Christmas. We had held our annual Christmas warehouse sale in Porchester Hall, off Queensway, since our own premises were no longer big enough for the many hundreds of people who came. It had become a major event. A beautifully decorated enormous Christmas tree had welcomed the shoppers in the foyer, where helium balloons for the children filled the ceiling and refreshments and mulled wine were available.

The event took planning, organization and lots of energy. There were 31 items on my to-do list, including sorting out the mulled wine, checking that we had helium for the balloons, making sure there were enough tills and staff, and ensuring that the clothes were priced properly.

Once the sale was done, there was the usual rush to buy presents and food and do all the last-minute things necessary in order to close the business for nearly two weeks. No wonder I was tired.

Work aside, I had become a grandmother. William and Samantha had become parents, and now I was babysitting my seven-month-old grandson, Saul, in between visits to Dad, whose health was deteriorating.

Given how much there was on my plate, I decided on the least complicated route for our spring show, which was once again to appear in the official venue in the tents in front of the Natural History Museum. I wasn't thrilled about this; I would have liked to do something more exciting, but I simply didn't have the energy to think about an alternative venue. So in February 2004, we presented our next winter collection, with a great deal of help from our brilliant new stylist, Cathy Kasterine. With her input it was a good show, and at the end I came out with Amy. Once again we were ignored by the trade press, but this time I refrained from wasting my time writing a letter I would never send.

Not long after this, Dad's girlfriend called me. He had taken a turn for the worse and was back in hospital. I dropped everything and rushed over there, finding him barely conscious and surrounded by nurses sticking needles into him. I could sense him wincing. I tried talking to him, but I had no idea if he heard me. I asked them to stop torturing him; we could all see that the needles were in vain. Dad had passed away.

I was sad, but not devastated as I had been when my mother died. Dad was 83 and his death was not unexpected. The funeral was held in the humanist chapel attached to Kensal Green Cemetery, where he was buried in the same grave as my mother. I invited his old friends and colleagues to the service, and they all reminisced about the past and said lovely funny things about him. The reception after the funeral was held at his flat, with refreshments provided by Albert Clark, who had started a private catering business after the restaurant he'd had with William closed. My lovely Andrew and my children were a fantastic support to me, and together we raised a glass to my infuriating, impossible, lovable father.

Claudia's wedding to Atticus Ross, August 2005.

Chapter Seventeen

The Runaway Train

It was 15 January 2005, my sixtieth birthday, and I was lying in bed thinking about getting up when Andrew came in with a bunch of beautiful red roses and a little velvet box. As I opened it, he asked me to marry him. Inside was a bespoke, one-of-a-kind ring, set with a yellow sapphire and diamonds in hand-carved gold. He told me he had designed it in collaboration with Ming Lampson, a talented young jewellery designer.

I gave him the biggest hug and kiss and said 'Yes, of course I will marry you'. My love for Andrew, and his for me, had never been in question. We had been together 13 years, and he had been at my side through all the challenges, problems and emotional upheavals I had gone through. A wedding seemed like the perfect next step, and being engaged made me feel loved and warm inside, but with everything that was going on, including my father's death and the rawness of my new-found sobriety, we both felt we were not ready to take that step quite yet. So we celebrated being engaged and spent a wonderful day together.

By coincidence, a few months later Claudia announced that she and Atticus were getting married. They wanted a wedding to remember and were going to have it in the grounds of the manor house at Ashby St Ledgers in Northamptonshire. The manor, which belonged to a friend of theirs, was famous for being the house where the Gunpowder Plot to assassinate King James I had been planned in 1605.

This was perfect. A lovely family wedding to enjoy, just not mine – yet. My team at Ghost made Claudia the most beautiful dress, fitted above the waist and gently flowing from the waist down. Delicate silver embroidery sewn on by hand made it totally unique. She looked stunning. The reception was to take place in the grounds, but rather than having a marquee, we decided on a 12-room yurt, with a central room big enough for a stage, a dance floor and all the tables. A friend of mine had a company called Eat Your Heart Out, which catered for famous musicians at festivals. Her team decorated the whole area beautifully, including the smaller rooms in the yurt, and provided a banquet meriting several Michelin stars.

Claudia and Atticus took their vows in a Norman church a short walk from the yurt. After everyone had enjoyed the banquet, it was time for the father of the bride to make a speech.

Michael got up on stage with his guitar and started singing a collection of father–daughter-themed songs, including 'Take Good Care of My Baby' and 'Lawdy Miss Clawdy'. After that he started playing a Janis Joplin song, 'Me and Bobby McGee'. He was really enjoying himself and showed no signs of stopping, despite his audience getting distinctly fidgety, so I asked William to gently nudge him off the stage before he could launch into another number.

After Michael, the family and friends band took over. This consisted of Atticus's brothers, Milo on vocals and Leo on guitar; his cousin Louis on guitar; Migi, a friend from Curiosity Killed the Cat, on drums; and Wayne Binitie on keyboards. Wayne had been in 12 Rounds with Claudia, but had gone on to pursue his love of art. He eventually became a Ph.D student at the Royal College of Art and a few years ago had an exhibition called Polar Zero at the UN Framework Convention on Climate Change. Andrew played drums on the first few songs, including 'Big Love' by Fleetwood Mac, and after Milo had sung a few numbers, Claudia came on and sang 'Islands in the Stream'. In a fantastic finale, she and Grace Jones duetted on 'Pull Up to the Bumper'.

Later there was a firework display, to highlights Atticus had put together from Gustav Holst's *The Planets*, followed by music and dancing until dawn.

My children's weddings were so different, and yet both so memorable. William and Samantha's was improvised, dramatic and chaotic, whereas Claudia and Atticus's was planned, beautiful and almost traditional. At the time of my son's wedding, I was fresh out of rehab and feeling very frail, so while I was equally touched and happy for him, the timing meant that I wasn't able to throw myself into celebrating in the same way that I could at Claudia's, where I danced the night away with Andrew while beaming at both my grown-up married children with enormous love and pride.

The wedding had preoccupied me for months, as I threw myself into organizing it – a wonderful distraction not just from my huge workload, but from the aftermath of my father's death, which carried on for months, as I'd had to sort out his possessions, arrange for probate and sell his flat to pay the unavoidable death duties.

Clearing his flat proved to be a nightmare. There were thousands of books, letters and photographs. I tried to give the books to universities, libraries, schools and charities, but no one would take them. He had such a wide range, from Tolstoy to biographies of African dictators, some of which he himself had written. I couldn't bear to throw them away, so I packed them up in boxes and put them in storage, hoping to find a home for them one day.

After the books, I began going through the letters, many of which were between my mother and her lover, a man called Nelson. My father had spent close on ten years in West Africa, setting up radio stations for Reuters along with other mysterious jobs for various governments out there. He would come back at irregular intervals, but sometimes we didn't see him for two or three years. In his absence, my mother had fallen in love with a Brazilian professor, and at one stage had moved him into our flat. I must have been 14 or 15 at the time, and I had no understanding of the love and affection she longed for. I had been horrible to him and asked him to leave. Going through the letters now, I understood why she loved Nelson, who clearly showed her the tenderness she craved. It also became clear that she had wanted to leave my father, but a sense of duty had stopped her.

I was in a quandary. Should I keep all these wonderful, heart-rending letters, or throw them away? No one else would ever want or have the time to read them, and yet it was impossible for me to get rid of them, so I kept some of the most poignant ones.

I made other discoveries going through the boxes of papers and letters. I found my grandmother's Women's Legion certificate dated 1916, and I discovered that my father's French aunt, who when I was 12 had arranged for me to stay with a family in France, had been a messenger for the French resistance. At the time I had thought her kind but unexciting. How wrong I was.

While I was preoccupied with my father's affairs, Claudia's wedding, and Ghost's new designs and upcoming shows, Ris had begun looking for investors for our business.

I trusted Ris completely. He was part-owner of Ghost, and his business head was far better than mine. But, distracted by other things, I wasn't paying enough attention. The two of us should have been working on the future of the company together, but I left many decisions to him. For years I had known exactly what was happening on the financial side, but at this point my focus was elsewhere. And it was because of this lack of attention that subsequent events turned into a runaway train ride that became impossible to stop.

Ris had decided we needed investment to expand the business and open more shops. This was perfectly reasonable. We had always expanded, but at this stage, with wholesale orders lower than they had once been, growing the business required a partner, one we could trust, who shared our vision and believed in Ghost the way we did.

With hindsight, I might have done things differently – perhaps cut our overheads, kept the business relatively small, but healthy and self-sufficient. But I didn't say a word and

I allowed the momentum to continue in the direction of investment.

It's painful, even now, to admit this, but I think my heart and soul were no longer totally in Ghost. It had been my baby, my pride and joy, for so long. But along with the distractions and my rehabilitation, two things had changed that powerfully influenced the way I felt.

The first, and most significant, was taking our manufacturing out of the UK. I had been so proud of using home manufacturers, and the work we gave them supported many families. When we took it away, they were devastated, and so was I. It didn't feel right or fair, but to survive we had to do it. And somehow nothing had felt quite the same since.

The second change was that the joy I had experienced in developing our perfumes had also gone, since I found it impossible to work with Procter & Gamble. Creating the perfumes had been fun, exciting and different. I had discovered a new talent and I would have loved to continue. But it wasn't to be, and things fell a little flat when it ended.

I still got a kick out of doing shows and I loved finding new talent and showcasing their designs. If I had a nose for perfume, I had a nose for fashion talent too, and I used it. When our lovely designer, Amy, left to have her second child, I went to see the brilliant Louise Wilson, who headed the

MA in Fashion course at Central Saint Martins. She offered to act as a consultant, which did help us, but she wasn't a designer, so I asked her to send us her most brilliant designer from the year that had just graduated. She sent us Yong Hei Fong, who had been mentored by Alexander McQueen. He was delightful as well as talented, and we had fun together. His innovative designs enhanced the femininity of the Ghost ethos, with ultra-soft fluidity in all the looks. The autumn/winter show was well received by the audience in the tent, and applause rang out as he and I came out together at the end. We had given it our all, and I felt optimistic. But despite the strength of the show, our wholesale orders remained static.

All these factors came into play as Ris took me from one meeting to another, in which big players in the fashion business discussed the company's future. Philip Green, who was yet to receive his knighthood, likened Ghost clothing to nightwear, which was typical of his lack of sophistication on matters of fashion.

We went to see Turkish fashion retail entrepreneur Touker Suleyman, who many years later would become a member of the panel on TV's *Dragons' Den*. He owned a factory and dye plant in Turkey, and Marks & Spencer had moved production of their Ghost range to his factories when Coats Viyella closed. Touker had produced the range for a year, until our collaboration with Marks came to an end when the new head of the company insisted that the Ghost name be on the clothes and we refused. During that year, he had learned all about our boiling, shrinking and dying process. He also knew that he could produce Ghost clothes more cheaply than we could, though I doubted the quality would be quite the same.

Touker made it clear that he wanted to buy Ghost, but the company was not for sale. Even if it had been, we would have turned him down, since he said he would have made most of our staff redundant and moved all Ghost production into his own premises.

We continued looking for investment, meeting the owners of Warehouse and Oasis, among others, plus representatives from an Icelandic group called Arev, which was working with Kevin Stanford. He was the former partner and husband of Karen Millen, and together they had built the hugely successful Karen Millen brand. After they separated, Kevin had gone on to become a major investor in a number of businesses, often partnering with Icelandic companies. His second wife was Icelandic, and he had a home in Reykjavik.

Kevin and Arev were seriously interested in Ghost. They told us they would open a thousand shops worldwide and make it a huge global brand. But to do this they wanted control, which meant owning 51 per cent of the business.

Kevin, along with several of the Arev group, attended the September 2005 show in London. It was an excellent show. Yong Fong was involved in the designs, Amy was back, and the show fizzed with energy and bright ideas. At the end, Yong Fong, Amy, Sophia and I came out together. The visitors were impressed.

Two months after the show, we signed a contract with Arev. I was uncomfortable about the idea of selling such a big stake, but we were given all kinds of reassurances. The contract stated that I would remain as managing director, Ris would continue as finance director and all the staff would be kept on. After all, together we were Ghost; without us, without me, they would simply be buying a name.

The agreement was that our new partners would join us at the start of 2006, concentrating on the retail side and opening shops. It made sense, and while I can't pretend that deep down there were no misgivings, I believed it would work. I wouldn't have signed with them otherwise. I wanted Ghost to flourish and I wanted to stay at the helm.

Our staff knew what was going on. I don't think they were happy about it, but they were philosophical about the situation since they understood that this was the best way for them to keep their jobs.

After our Christmas warehouse sale at Porchester Hall,

I booked a restaurant in Wigmore Street, and we held a celebration dinner with the Ghost staff and our new partners. It was all slightly awkward, since the Ghosties were inhibited by the strangers in our midst, and everyone was on their best behaviour. Our parties were usually so relaxed and full of fun; watching the discomfort of this occasion, I wondered if we hadn't made a terrible mistake. If we had, it was too late, so I did my best to put the thought out of my mind. I told myself that we could, and would, make it work. It might take time for everyone to get used to the new arrangement, but while some things changed, much would remain as it had been and we would go on as we had before.

I spent Christmas in Ramsgate with Andrew and returned to Ghost HQ after the break energized and optimistic. Our future was secured, and now the focus was on the new designs for autumn and winter, which would be shown in February. Everyone was busy, the atmosphere was as full of energy as it had ever been, and the usual questions about everything from design to accessories to sales were never-ending.

I hadn't taken much notice of a woman who had appeared behind a desk in our workspace. Kevin told me she was there to look after the retail side of the business, and that was fine; retail was what they had said they would focus on. I did try to make polite conversation with her on a few occasions, but she was surprisingly unfriendly. I was puzzled; why wouldn't she want to get on with me? But with so much to do, I didn't dwell on it.

Our show that February was excellent. I loved the designs that Yong Fong, Amy and Sophia had created, and we had taken on a new stylist, Karl Plewka – who was also a friend of mine – who helped enormously. I'm so glad the show was such a success, because it turned out to be my last one, though I had no idea at the time.

The days of riotous Ghost after-show parties were over, but we still wanted to celebrate a great show, so we went to a local pub. The new woman in the office had come to the show, but in the pub she ignored me. Once again, I was puzzled, and a little hurt. Surely we needed to cooperate and work together to make this new venture successful? The Ghosties were such a strong, functional team, I didn't want anything to spoil that.

If only I'd had an inkling of what was really going on. But I did not.

A few days after the show, I walked into work to find the new woman rearranging the showroom and dismissing certain collection pieces. When I asked her what she was doing, she replied that she was the new managing director, in charge of retail. I was shocked. I had imagined that I was the only managing director; were there now two of us?

I made a valiant attempt to work with her. I asked her into a private area, and calmly, in the nicest way possible, suggested that if we were going to have to collaborate on a daily basis, we should try to have a better working relationship to make the business function at its best. I asked her to shake hands on this, but she refused, and walked out. I told Ris, but he said to simply ignore her and that I was managing director as per the contract.

The following week, I was summoned to Kevin Stanford's office in Bond Street, where Arev had their headquarters. I hoped he would explain how things were going to work between me and the new woman. To my horror, he said tersely that he was putting me on gardening leave, and I was to return to Ghost, collect my personal possessions and leave the building immediately. I didn't understand. What was gardening leave? For the first time ever in my life, I was lost for words.

Why didn't I shout at him? Why didn't I ask him what the hell was he talking about? I was managing director, so how could he order me out? I have asked myself many times why I didn't challenge him. But the shock was such that I was stunned. I couldn't talk. Disbelief and powerlessness overwhelmed me.

I left his office barely able to think straight. I felt sick and my stomach was turning over. How could this be happening? It was barely three months since we had agreed the deal with Arev, and now it appeared that I was losing everything. Ghost was my baby, my creation. Arev had given me so many promises about the future of the company, our future, my future. I couldn't grasp what had just happened. Totally numb, I went back to the office as if I was sleepwalking.

When they heard what had happened, my team and the rest of the staff were as shocked as I was. There was silence as I gathered a few personal things and my laptop. When I walked out of the building a few minutes later, no one was working. It was as though they had all become statues, rooted to the spot where they sat or stood.

Thankfully Andrew was at home. He made me a cup of tea as I wept at the kitchen table. He had always advised caution in dealing with what he saw as cold-blooded investors on a hunting trip. But he also recognized the precarious situation Ghost was in.

My emotions for the next few days were all over the place. I was devastated, disbelieving, angry, heartbroken. I blamed myself, then Arev, then myself again. Why hadn't I understood that they could do this to me?

The one thing I am hugely proud of is that throughout this horribly painful time, I did not turn to alcohol or drugs. Copious amounts of tea and boxes of tissues, but that was it.

After I had left the office, a horrified Ris had got on the phone to the boss of Arev, who told him that they didn't want me involved in the business and wanted to buy the remaining 49 per cent of Ghost. Ris rang to tell me this, and when I had calmed down enough to be relatively rational, he and I discussed the situation.

Part of me wanted to go in guns blazing and sue for wrongful dismissal. After all, I had a signed contract stating that I would continue to be managing director. But at the same time, I dreaded the prospect of getting bogged down in employment litigation, and given that we would be a minion up against a juggernaut with bottomless funds, I would in all likelihood lose. At the very least they could drag it out for years. Painful as the realization was, I needed to move on.

Ris didn't want to stay at Ghost without me, and most of the staff agreed with him. With aching hearts we decided to take the money they were offering for the remaining 49 per cent. When Ris relayed this to the Ghost staff, all of them, with only two exceptions, said they wouldn't work for the new people. Their loyalty made me very proud.

Under the new contract, Ris was to stay on for a short while to show Arev how everything worked, and I agreed not to work in the fashion business for one year. I was allowed to come in once more to say goodbye to the staff and to collect any personal possessions I had not already taken. I took all the books containing the thousands of colours I had painted while gazing at the sea in Ramsgate. They belonged to me, not to Ghost. Ris also promised to gather all the press cuttings and press books and smuggle them out to me.

Claudia came with me to the warehouse where we stored the clothes. It was located in a separate building that belonged to me personally, since I had bought the lease with the money left me by my father. Together we filled black bags with as many show pieces as we could find. The new people had no use for them anyway, and the pieces meant so much to me.

And that, so to speak, was that. My wonderful Ghost was gone. It had all happened so quickly that it left me distraught and in deep mourning. The company I had founded, worked for, loved so much and fought so hard for had been taken from under me. Once again, I was lost.

Getting my OBE, 2010. Photograph by Charles Green.

Chapter Eighteen

From the Ashes

I hated the idea of being barred from working in the fashion industry for a year, but my sabbatical year, as I called it, turned out to be a bonus. It allowed me to rest, something I hadn't done for many years, to get fit and to think about what I wanted to do next.

Every day I would walk and run the half-hour or so from my house to Wormwood Scrubs Park, cross the green where the American school played their baseball matches and exercise on the outdoor equipment, before walking and running home. I lost all the weight I had put on since I stopped drinking and got fitter than I had been for many years.

Best of all, I got to spend a lot of time with my first grandchild, Saul. William and Samantha had started an organic child-friendly burger restaurant on Portobello Road called Babes'n'Burgers, which took up all their energy and time, plus Samantha was pregnant with their second child, but here was Granny Tanya with time on her hands and a lot more patience with a three-year-old than I'd had when I was a mum. I loved this year with Saul. He had a little pushbike, and when we went out, he would weave in and out of shop aisles and people on the street while telling me that 'water is the best drink of the day', with which I concurred. He never wanted to leave Granma and Grandrew, as he called Andrew, when his dad came to fetch him to take him home.

Andrew was now making a range of programmes for BBC's Radio 4 and other networks with his independent production company Curtains For Radio, which he had worked hard to establish. We loved the extra time we had together, as well as the time we spent with little Saul.

We had many happy times during that year. Isiah was born in July, and after meeting our second beautiful little grandson, Andrew and I rushed over to Los Angeles to meet our third – Claudia and Atticus's son, Lucius, born in the same month.

We took most of the expensive vintage furnishings from the Ghost shop, which the new owners, despite having said they would open a thousand shops worldwide, had closed, and gave them to Claudia and Atticus. Later on, we also had a proper holiday, my first for many years, in Denmark.

We decided to spend the money I had received for the enforced sale of Ghost on a house in the countryside. After much searching, we thought we had found the perfect one. It was a manor house in a small village in Wiltshire, an hour and a half from our London home. It was close to Salisbury Plain, where the army practised manoeuvres, and had belonged to the Ministry of Defence. During the First World War it had been used as a hospital and convalescent centre for wounded Canadian soldiers, and after the war, various army officers had lived in it for brief periods.

The MoD had sold it for next to nothing to Nomura, a Japanese bank, from whom we bought it. It was unusual in having a thatched roof and beautiful high ceilings inside, but it was in a state of disrepair. The army had put a second layer of wallpaper over damp walls, or in some cases built new stud walls to go in front of damp walls. Fireplaces had been made regulation size, and every room had a washbasin, but there wasn't one shower. Time to call Ted, who came to our rescue and installed a workforce. The work had to be done with care, and there were limitations on what we could do, because it was a Grade II listed building. But gradually the inside took shape, and outside there was plenty of room for a tennis court, which after much negotiating with the local council we were allowed to construct. Our weekends became full of countryside rather than sea, and Ramsgate became a family heirloom for our children and grandchildren.

There was one more task I had to accomplish in my year off, and that was to give up smoking. I was dreading it; I had smoked since the age of 14, which was not far off 50 years. I did some research and found a rehabilitation centre for smokers run by Seventh-day Adventists in the wine-growing district near San Francisco. I booked the week-long course and set off for my second bout of rehab.

The centre was more like a hotel than my previous rehab. We were taken hiking at 7 am, and then, after breakfast – all the meals were vegetarian – we had lectures and were taught how to reroute the paths in our brains, much like ring roads around a town. Among the other penitent smokers were a lawyer, a bored New York housewife, a physical trainer, a dancer, a croupier, a journalist and a telephone salesman who kept a case of Jack Daniel's in his room. They were a motley, friendly crew; we got on well and played volleyball in the small pool when we had breaks.

At the end of the week, we gathered in a circle, promising to keep in touch and not to smoke. No one kept in touch, and news from the centre some months later informed me that out of the 12 of us, only the journalist and I had managed not to have that first cigarette. I never smoked again, but I did become hooked on Nicorette Fruitfusion chewing gum. My lungs may be clear of smoke, but nicotine continues to rewire my brain – for now. I am planning to do something about this very soon.

Towards the end of my enforced sabbatical year, I became itchy; my desire to work again was growing daily, if not hourly, and I began secret talks with two of my former staff. Sophia Malig, my wonderful designer and right hand, had started teaching part-time at Winchester School of Art, and Neil Smith, a great pattern cutter, was teaching part-time at Central Saint Martins.

On a trip to New York, I had discovered Gary Graham, a truly talented designer. I had fallen in love with his work, which echoed the Ghost design ethic of bias-cut femininity but was more innovative, asymmetric and modern. I had asked him if he would design a collection for the new company I was about to start. He had agreed to work long-distance, in much the same way Andrea had when I started Ghost.

Once Sophia and Neil agreed to join me, I got in touch with other Ghost staff who had left after the takeover and who I believed would work well in my new enterprise. They were all keen to come on board. What are you going to call your new label? they asked. I had thought about this and had come up with the name Handwritten. To me, the word epitomized everything Ghost had been about; it was a very hands-on, labour-intensive, individual collection. I trademarked the name and continued to plan my next move.

I knew exactly where we would set up our workspace. After Ris had bulldozed my little isolation office in the middle of the old marble works, we'd constructed a new building in its footprint with a studio on the upper floor and warehouse space below. A bridge led to Ghost HQ in the Chapel, and the new owners were currently using both buildings. Ghost owned the Chapel but not this building, which belonged to the pension fund, so I claimed ownership of it and gave them one month's notice to move out. Gosh, that felt good.

I'd heard rumours that the unfriendly woman who had replaced me had got rid of everything that reminded her of me. She'd changed all the furniture and fittings, while the staff who had been brought in to replace the loyal Ghosties who'd walked out in my wake were apparently only allowed to communicate with each other via their computers and email. Imagine staff who aren't allowed to speak to one another! The atmosphere sounded like the absolute opposite of what it had formerly been. It sounded miserable.

Once the new people had moved out of the building – somewhat ungraciously – we moved in, cleaned the space and got to work. Our first collection was basically a follow-up from where I had left off at Ghost, except that Gary's designs

Handwritten lookbook photo taken by Nick Haddow.

were more asymmetric and modern, with multiple zips and mixed fabrics within each garment. We continued with bias cuts and used all the Ghost fabrics, which I bought from our old supplier.

Andrew and Ris said Handwritten was my revenge, and perhaps there is a grain of truth in this, but in all honesty, I can say that that wasn't what motivated me. I had always worked, I needed to work, I loved a challenge, and I loved fashion. I wasn't the kind of person who could stay at home, lunch with girlfriends, visit the beauty salon and achieve nothing.

The first collection sold to many of our old customers and did well. However, I made two big mistakes. The first was to market the collection under Gary's name. No one in the UK had ever heard of him, whereas I had made a name for myself and was known. This wasn't helpful; we couldn't get the press to take note, and some buyers, not understanding that I was behind the label, didn't take the time to come and look at the collection.

The other mistake I made was to work with a former Ghost salesperson. She agreed to sell Handwritten if she could bring the other labels she was now selling with her. She told me that the showroom looked a bit empty with just Handwritten. The brands she was selling were all good, high-quality ones, so I agreed, and we named it Showroom West 10. But after the second season, more collections appeared, and Handwritten was suddenly fighting for space. It was all too much. Showroom West 10 was dissolved, and Handwritten could breathe again with the space to ourselves.

While I immersed myself in Handwritten and was loving every minute, Ghost was in trouble. I can't pretend I didn't leap with joy when I heard the news that the company was insolvent and had declared bankruptcy. It was hard not to crack a smile. I wondered how much it had cost in terms of money, time and energy to remove any traces of me, which by all accounts they had been determined to do. By being so heavy-handed, they had also obliterated the style, the ethos and the energy that had made Ghost so special. All they had left was the name.

Ris and I discussed the possibility of buying the company back. But it had been so trashed in those two years that we knew it would need a massive investment to restore it to where it had been. The owners had also raised money by mortgaging the Chapel, so it was doubtful whether it would even have a home to return to. Besides which, Ris was now working for the daughters of Body Shop founder Anita Roddick, and I was a year into Handwritten. Neither of us wanted to go backwards in our lives, so we decided to let Ghost go its own way, without us interfering. Touker Suleyman, who had wanted the company for a long time, bought it from the liquidators minus the perfume, which stayed with Procter & Gamble.

While I watched these proceedings with some interest, and sadness too, I concentrated on building Handwritten. I needed a really good salesperson, and I found one in Anton Meyer, a tall South African. I had met him years before, when he worked as a buyer for a shop I had sold to in the early days of Ghost. Anton was patient, charming, persuasive, very hard-working and he knew all sides of the business. I decided to give fashion shows a miss; I didn't have the staff or the finance, and I had done enough of them. Besides, things had moved on since the days of the fun, exciting shows. Instead, Anton and I decided to visit the trade fairs in Paris and New York.

Gary Graham did two collections for us, but he didn't like the extra work required to modify his designs to make them more commercial. He also didn't like coming to London twice a year. He left Handwritten to go into theatrical design, but not before he had given us a fabulous start that we could take further on our own. I am very proud of many of the Handwritten pieces. I have more Handwritten in my wardrobe today than I do Ghost.

After Gary, we worked on a freelance basis with two or three other designers, each of whom would offer one good idea, which we developed. Sophia contributed greatly, introducing knitwear, lacy thermals and jersey pants that I still live in.

We managed to break even, but it was challenging. The credit crisis hit in 2008, making business far more precarious. Suddenly everything involved much harder work, with fewer rewards. Added to this, so much had changed in the fashion world. There were hundreds more designers, and many of the outlets I had sold to before had closed. A lot of fashion businesses were going online, but I wasn't great at selling this way. Life at Ghost had been fun for the staff, with outings, big bonuses courtesy of the warehouse sales and good salaries. Now margins were smaller and there was no room for complacency or for extras.

Perhaps because we had put in so much effort, we were especially thrilled to receive the Newcomers Export Award at the UK Fashion and Textile Export Awards of 2010. It was presented by Joanna Lumley, and it lifted all our spirits.

Meanwhile, William and Samantha had their third child, Azura, in July, and in September, Claudia and Atticus had Ione. Two little granddaughters to add to the fold! Absolute joy for all of us.

The other significant event of 2010 was the arrival of a letter from the Royal Household informing me that I was to be awarded an OBE for my services to the fashion industry in the Queen's Honours List. I was stunned. I wasn't known for toeing the line – I was the bad girl who answered back to authority, and was known as the Queen of Parties – so to receive this honour was truly unexpected, and I couldn't help but be thrilled. All my hard work had been given recognition. WOW!

The ceremony was not for another six months, so I had plenty of time to bask in the pleasure of anticipation. It didn't last long. In December of that year, I noticed that my eyesight had been doing strange things. Objects in my vision had begun to look flattened, squashed and elongated. I went to a clever optician in Salisbury, who immediately knew that something was wrong and sent me to a specialist in London. In February, I was diagnosed with a pituitary adenoma – a brain tumour. Thankfully it wasn't malignant, but as it grew, it was pushing up against the optic chiasm, where my optic nerve ran, distorting my vision. I would need surgery to remove it, and the surgeon would need to go through my nose and sinuses to get at the culprit.

I was shaken, but I knew it could have been so much worse. I was whisked into hospital, where a surgeon performed a transsphenoidal adenomectomy. The operation took four to five hours, but went well. It really wasn't that much of an ordeal, except that I was unable to celebrate with Andrew on the publication of his first book, which came out the day after my operation. It was called *I Was Douglas Adams's Flatmate*. Faber had asked him to write it based on a series he had done for Radio 4 in which he interviewed individuals who had been close to famous artists during a significant period in their careers.

I recovered well, which I put down to the fact that I was fit and no longer smoking or drinking, and was soon back at work.

On 28 June 2011, wearing a Handwritten dress and sequinned cardigan, complemented by a hat from Stephen Jones and accompanied by Andrew, William and Claudia, I set off for Buckingham Palace. The ceremony was short and sweet. I told the Queen that her daughter had visited my business, but the handshake she gave me told me that was enough, and I barely had time to say thank you. What an amazing woman, and what a sense of duty. She had to shake hands with about 150 people every two weeks, and she didn't even wear gloves. Afterwards Claudia and Andrew informed me that the band playing in the background was a little out of tune, which made me laugh. I bought all the paraphernalia associated with the event, and the smiling pictures of the four of us are a lovely reminder.

A year later, in the summer of 2011, I went for an MRI scan and a check-up and was told that the tumour had returned. I went back into hospital and had a second operation. I prayed that the nasty little weed, as I decided to call it, had learned its lesson and wouldn't grow again, and after a couple of weeks I went back to work.

Handwritten kept going for the next couple of years, producing lovely clothes and turning over a million pounds a year, which sounds impressive but was actually only just enough to keep the company afloat, if I didn't pay myself anything. It certainly didn't allow for pay rises or expansion. I asked myself why the money situation was so tight when our overheads were relatively low. The reason, it turned out, was that we had accumulated far too much stock. Fabric had to be ordered in advance of sales, to meet delivery times, and mistakes had been made by one of my staff when placing orders and writing up dockets.

The excess stock had to be turned into money, so I went to Portobello Road and scoured the area for a shop to rent. I found a few, but none of the estate agents would consider anything less than a three-year lease. I wanted three months. Then I got lucky. I spotted a shop in a perfect position, at the upmarket end of Portobello Road, between Elgin and Blenheim Crescents. I rang the agent handling it, and he told me that his wife loved Ghost; she had even got married in a Ghost dress. He said I could have the shop for three months.

It was in good condition, and after a thorough clean, we put in rails, and three makeshift changing rooms, draped with our fabrics. I had a sign made for the window saying: 'For a limited time only – vintage Ghost and Handwritten'. When the new owners of Ghost had thrown out our original fibreglass mannequins, which lit up from inside, I'd managed to retrieve a couple, and I put them in the window.

Along with the excess Handwritten stock, I had the Ghost show pieces that Claudia and I had piled into black bags during our warehouse raid. We filled the rails, and my daughter-in-law, Samantha, offered to work in the shop, along with Miya, who had been modelling for Handwritten in the showroom. They were joined by one of our new designers, El.

I had first met El when I was invited to Falmouth School of Art to give a lecture on fashion. She was introduced to me as their star pupil, and later she came to Handwritten for an internship, before going off to Sri Lanka to do her own collection. When she came back three months later, she worked for me again, designing and filling in wherever she was needed. El was in her late twenties, tall, slim and beautiful. She was also a lovely, gentle, caring person, and hugely talented. She became, and still is, one of my closest friends.

The shop did brilliantly from the word go. When we opened, Touker Suleyman phoned me to say he was taking legal action, since I had no business having a Ghost shop. I explained politely that it wasn't a Ghost shop, it was a shop selling some vintage Ghost pieces, which any shop had a right to do. I wished him luck and put the phone down.

Selling the stock and vintage Ghost eased our financial pressure, but back in the Handwritten studio and offices, things were not going well. Upstairs there was friction between the pattern cutter and the machinist, and downstairs between the person invoicing and the person sending out orders. And our accountant was having non-stop problems with our freelance bookkeeper.

Despite all of this, we continued to produce beautiful clothes. In the spring of 2014, Anton and I took the collection to Paris. Tranoï was regarded as the best of several key trade shows, and was difficult to get into, such was the competition, so we were fortunate to be showing there. It took place in one of the most beautiful old Parisian buildings. As always, we greeted some old customers and welcomed new ones, but I was sinking into a strange depression. I remember being on our stand and thinking, what the hell am I doing here? I've had enough. I looked around me at the familiar faces and fake smiles, all trying to sell their collections, and thought, this isn't me any longer. I'm nearly 70. It's time to get out.

On my return to London, I went to see my son. He knew everyone and everything that was going on locally. I told him I had had enough and wanted to close the business and sell the building, so would he ask around, discreetly, for someone looking for a large commercial property. Lo and behold, a week later, a young man came into the office and said he had heard from William that I might want to sell. He told me he was looking for a building suitable for a couple of sound studios and offices.

I showed him around and he told me he liked what he saw and would talk to his music business client and get back to me.

That same day, Neil, my pattern cutter, gave in his notice, saying that he could no longer work with our machinist. And Anton announced that he was engaged, and that he and his husband planned to return to South Africa. I didn't say a word, I just prayed that the young man interested in the building would come back with his client. Business was hard enough, but without Anton and Neil, I would have needed a whole lot more energy and determination than I had.

As luck would have it, the young man phoned me and made an appointment to view the property with his client's brother, who decided it was perfect and offered me almost double the amount it had cost to build it. It was a great deal for the pension fund, and a great deal for the client, musician Guy Chambers, since the property has certainly increased in value since then.

There was one sale condition: we had to move out by the end of the month, which gave us less than three weeks. Since we were in the middle of shipping our orders, this was a nightmare. However, it was too good a price to turn down. Somehow we had to do it.

Thankfully the staff weren't a problem. Most were freelance, with only a small handful employed by me, so they accepted my decision calmly and rose to the task magnificently. Angela

Bradley, who had been a Ghostie since early on, finished all the invoicing, and lovely Russell who had worked for me for many years, dealt with the packing, quality control and shipping. Sophia insisted on coming with me wherever we went, to tie up all the loose ends and wind the business up, and El also stayed to help in any way she could.

We sold our sewing machines, leftover fabric and pattern-cutting table for a song, after which I managed to secure a monthly tenancy on two small offices a few minutes' walk away from Handwritten, owned by the local council. They were damp, and when it rained, water coursed around the building through noisy gutters, while the main railway line into Paddington from the west was less than 12 feet from the back wall. But a monthly tenancy was a rare find, so we gritted our teeth, packed up all the Handwritten paraphernalia – books, files, computers, patterns – in double-quick time and managed to move out of the Handwritten building with a day to spare.

We settled into our depressing new offices, and in spite of endless trains thundering past and the frequent gurgle of rainwater, over the next three months we managed to complete the admin involved in winding up a business. I needed to advise all the shops and individual customers that we were closing. An illustrator friend of mine, Bridget MacKeith, made a card with a cartoon of me surrounded by clothes, and I wrote a personal note to all our customers thanking them for their loyalty.

I was amazed at the many heart-warming replies I received from women who had bought our clothes, thanking me for the pleasure I had given them over the years, telling me how much they would treasure the garments they had and that they would miss not being able to buy new ones.

One email was from a man saying, 'Thank God you're closing, I can't afford any more of your clothes. My wife already has two cupboards full.' Another read, 'Please let Tanya Sarne know that, as a curvy woman, clothes from Ghost and Handwritten have been a lifesaver for me over the years and almost my whole wardrobe is made up of Ghost and Handwritten items. The slip dresses are just fantastic and so easy to accessorize, easy to wash, easy to wear and always stylish but in an edgy, understated way. Her clothes always make me feel contemporary, stylish, comfortable and chic. My friend and I hold Tanya in very high esteem and think the clothes she has produced over the years are in a class of their own.'

Replies like these made me cry. What better reward for my hard work than to have given pleasure to so many women.

Me and Andrew, married, outside the register office, 2015.

Chapter Nineteen

One Last Throw

I felt I was finished with the world of fashion. I'd run one hugely successful business and a second that did pretty well. My plan was to put my feet up and take it easy. But I hadn't reckoned on the intervention of Sherry.

Sherry had been around Ghost, and me, from the mid-nineties on, and we had stayed firm friends. But even so, when she came to visit me and suggested we start another label, I wasn't keen. She didn't give up, though; she came over several times to persuade me to dip just one tiny toe in the water again.

Over lunch in a vegan restaurant, she finally won me over. The new label, we agreed, was to be called Sarne. No more anonymity. I was convinced that the middle market of fashion, where I had always been, was saturated, so we decided that this would be more expensive and upmarket than any of my previous collections.

Before I could begin looking for premises, I had to go into hospital for a third operation. A check-up had revealed that the nasty little weed in my head was back. This time I was told that if it returned again, a fourth operation would be dangerous so I would have to undergo long and intensive radiotherapy instead.

On an earlier visit to Los Angeles to see Claudia and Atticus, Andrew had taken me to the John Wayne Cancer Institute to get a second opinion. Surrounded by a multitude of doctors, I had been told that they would have taken my pituitary gland out completely in the first surgery, so that no more operations would have been needed. Mentally I had thanked the British surgeon for trying to keep the vital little master gland that conducts and controls so many of the body's functions.

The day after my third surgery, I was lying in bed when my phone rang. The woman at the other end said she was writing a press release for a new clothing label called hw2. She explained that the two women behind the label had told her they had worked for me for many years and I was their mentor. She asked me for my comments and a quote. I told her I had just come out of surgery, and put the phone down.

While we were tying up the ends of Handwritten, I had noticed two of the remaining staff huddled away in corners having private conversations. I asked what was going on, and one of them told me that since Handwritten was closing, the two of them were thinking of carrying on under a different name. I have to admit I didn't take it very seriously. I suggested to them, as a joke, that they call it hw2, and then thought no more of it. But it seemed they had continued with their plan, misinterpreting my throwaway comment as approval.

I was more than annoyed. If they had asked if I minded the two of them carrying on the business, I would have felt differently, but they hadn't; they had simply gone ahead, believing I was OK with it. I had worked so hard to build it up, with everything that involved – from design to fabrics, production, clients and so much more – and here it was all laid out for them on a silver platter. Of course I was annoyed, and cross with myself that I had never put in place confidentiality contracts.

I decided to concentrate on my recovery and not my anger. Andrew was working, so William collected me, and I left hospital feeling fragile. Before I was discharged, I'd had to see an endocrinologist to find out which of my hormones needed replacing, given that the functions of my pituitary gland had been compromised. I was put on growth hormone, which required a daily injection, steroids and thyroxine. Lucky me.

Was I really going to start again with Sarne? I couldn't resist one last throw of the dice. I had always loved working, and in my weakened state I needed something to look forward to. While I was still recovering, I phoned several local commercial estate agents. The nearest I could get to Portobello Road, which had become very expensive and where there was nothing available, was Latimer Road. At the southern end were twin buildings, one of which was for sale. It wasn't particularly pretty on the outside, but inside it was very eighties and quite friendly.

It was on three floors, with no lift, but generous wide stairs and huge tinted windows throughout. I took the top floor for Sarne and let the other floors to an ex-tenant of mine who had rented the old Ghost warehouse after the sale of the company. They were called Money Clothing. I liked them and knew we would get along.

The top floor was open-plan, from the front of the building to the back. It became narrower in the middle, where the entrance was, so without the need for doors it divided into two main areas. I wanted to make the place comfortable, not only as our workspace but as overspill accommodation for Claudia and Atticus when they came over with Lucius and Ione.

I kept one toilet and turned the second into a shower room, installed a small kitchen in the back, and in the front put a comfortable leather double sofa bed complete with side tables, lights and a big TV. We decorated the front part with the antique mirrors, rugs, sofas and chairs we had kept in storage.

The sewing machines went into the back area, along with the leftover Handwritten stock, and we covered a table-tennis table with plastic sheeting, so no one walking in would have thought it was anything but a cutting table.

The workspace was gorgeous. Sherry joined me, and so did El, who was keen to be part of the new venture. Together we reasoned that if we worked hard, we could do in four days what was usually accomplished in five. Sherry had to come up from Brighton, and I did all my shopping on Fridays and then went to the country for the weekend, so a four-day week sounded perfect.

Ris would later tell me that Sarne was a hobby, not a business. He was probably right, but we did work hard, and we had no problem getting everything done in time.

Working there was a joy. We always had lovely lunches cooked by me or El. And we made very beautiful clothes. Sophia sent us a delightful young Japanese woman called Sumi who could cut patterns and sew, as could El. We had a huge library of fabrics to choose from. At Handwritten, I had continued to work with a factory in Romania we used in the last days of Ghost, and I enjoyed an excellent and close relationship with Katty, the owner.

In her warehouse, Katty had the fabrics from Ghost that had been sent there before it was taken over. She also had all the sampling from Handwritten, plus hundreds of metres left over from orders. She had made a file of all these numerous fabrics, with swatches and quantities, and sent it to me.

We concentrated on the more expensive fabrics. In the first season we used all the fabric with either gold embroidery or gold polka dots. My original idea was to do trans-seasonal collections. This made complete sense to me, but I couldn't single-handedly change the long-established habits of buyers, so we were left with no choice but to stick to the norm of spring/summer and autumn/winter.

None of us were into social media, so we lost out there, but we did have a website, and we received the occasional order through that. America was our main market, where we had a limited but consistent customer base who could afford our prices, so the only trade show we did was the Designers & Agents show in New York. El and I found a small but good hotel within walking distance of the venue, and Mina, who had worked for Ghost's former New York agents and was dating the bass player from the New York Dolls, joined us to help out. It was slow going, but it was fun, and New York was a welcome change from London.

Claudia and her children arrived in London shortly after Christmas to celebrate the start of 2015 and our January birthdays. I had been engaged to Andrew for ten years, and now he said, 'How about it?' I thought 70 seemed like a good age to get married, so I said yes.

On 9 January, six days before my seventieth birthday, we were married in Chelsea Old Town Hall. It was strictly a family affair, and a truly joyous occasion. El and Sherry dressed me up in Sarne clothes, and we shared the special day with my children and the grandchildren – Saul, now 11, Lucius and Isiah, both 8, and Azura and Ione, both 4.

Andrew's sister, Barbie, and Claudia's mother-in-law, Bunty, completed the guest list, plus a photographer. Saul, Lucius and Isiah argued about who would give Andrew the wedding ring. We recited 'The Owl and the Pussycat', and all five of the grandchildren sat almost on top of us as we signed the register. On the steps of the town hall, the children threw hundreds of rose petals over us, thanks to Claudia, and then we all went back to our house and had tea and cake. It was perfect.

A few days later, we had a big party to celebrate our marriage, my birthday on the 15th, my son-in-law's on the 16th (Atticus couldn't be there because of work, but we celebrated for him), and my daughter and daughter-in-law's on the 17th. We covered the garden at the back of the house as we had done for the millennium party, and installed a dance floor. The wonderful Eat your Heart Out team who had made my daughter's wedding so perfect cooked delicious food, and

Signing the marriage certificate, helped by all five grandchildren.

I added a chocolate fountain. The party was full to overflowing with friends, family and children, all having a wonderful time, when the police arrived at 11.30 pm to close us down. A neighbour had complained about the noise. I told the police it was a Saturday night and I had just got married. They gave us another hour until 12.30 am, and then we had to move proceedings inside.

A few months after the party, and a year after my third operation, I went for my annual check-up. It wasn't good news. The nasty little weed had found a comfortable home in my head and refused to go away no matter how much the surgeon cut it back or how rude I was to it. Surgery was no longer possible, so I would need a six-week course of radiotherapy at University College Hospital.

I told Sherry and El that my hours would be limited and began a daily trip to the hospital. Rory, who had been my last driver at Ghost and had since become a black cab driver, collected me every morning at ten, drove me to the hospital, waited for me in the licensed cab area and then drove me back to Sarne in time for lunch. His invaluable help saved me from having to take the Tube, possibly picking up an infection on the way. And as the treatment progressed, I needed this help, since every session made me progressively more exhausted.

I made friends with other patients who had similar treatment times to me. There was a wonderful middle-aged man, a master builder, who used to come in with a big smile on his face and say to me, 'Tanya, you got to stay positive.' He died not long after finishing his treatment, but his message was right.

When my course of radiotherapy was complete, I was allowed to keep the mask that had been fitted to my face. It currently decorates one of my mannequins, and is a constant reminder of how lucky I am to be alive.

I returned to work to find that our orders had grown; we now had two Dutch and one German customer, along with a handful of English ones. We worked with love, devotion and pride, but not a lot of money. However, I had kept the mortgage facility that I'd had at Handwritten, and our overheads were low, so finance wasn't a big problem. When we worked late, El often slept on the premises. The office was as comfortable as any good hotel room.

The three of us were friends, not just workmates, and we enjoyed our working days. We made lookbooks, containing pages with every style in a fabric and the price, and Sherry suggested we shoot a video showing the production process. We ended up making a very surreal film. We dressed Sumi in an oversized raw cloth dress, and she twirled round and round. This was speeded up to give the impression she was in a washing machine. At the end, she comes to a standstill and the dress now fits her perfectly, and is no longer stiff but flowing. A friend of El's shot it, and Claudia wrote the music. We put it on our website, but I think it was a little esoteric for most people. Much later, Sherry and El gave me a birthday present of three framed photos taken from this video, which hang proudly on a wall in our house.

The weekends in the country, which meant so much to me and Andrew, were becoming less enjoyable, thanks to our neighbours. One weekend, we found that a tractor had been driven over the tennis court. Our water bills came to thousands of pounds. We called the water company, and they discovered that someone had hijacked our supply. Although we were friendly towards our neighbours, the house had too much history with the military, and we were regarded as outsiders and somewhat eccentric, not least because we didn't keep the tradition of holding the annual church fete on our lawn.

Eventually we decided we had to sell, and began our search for another house. None of the properties we saw had the privacy and peace we wanted, and we had all but given up when we heard about a house in the New Forest, on the Hampshire border. It wasn't remarkable, or anywhere near as grand as the one we were selling, but it was totally private. It came with several acres of forest and was far enough away from any roads that all you could hear on summer evenings were the insects and birds. Andrew fell in love with it, and we put in an bid, only to be told we were too late; it was already under offer.

Andrew was devastated, but a few weeks later the estate agent called me to say that the buyers had withdrawn their offer after discovering that the land was a SINC, a Site of Importance for Nature Conservation, which meant that they would not be able to do anything with the forest except look after it.

We still hadn't sold our Wiltshire home, so we bought this one, using every penny we had plus a loan, and I furnished it incredibly cheaply by bidding online at an auction in the north of England, which I found very exciting.

Samantha, my daughter-in-law, took charge of renting the house out through Airbnb, and we saved the proceeds for restructuring and renovating it. A year later, we sold our Wiltshire home, at a considerable loss, to a lovely family who were perfect for it. At which point we stopped the Airbnb lets and I phoned Ted. Nine months later, with Ted's creativity, great builders, and money we couldn't afford, we ended up with the perfect home. We are there still, keepers of the forest, happy in our hideaway.

Most delivery vans have trouble finding the property as it falls between several postcodes. The Royal Mail van is the largest vehicle that can deliver anything to us, and the postman frequently asks, 'How's paradise today?' He is right. It really is paradise. As I look out of my window, two hares have just run across the lawn, and a group of fallow deer are nibbling the grass at the far end near the trees, while a pheasant cock tries to stand his ground with a rival.

By late 2016, when we were looking for a house, Sarne had been going for two years. Fashion stock inherited from Ghost and Handwritten was piling up, so we decided to have a sale. I asked an actress friend of mine, Mika Simmons, to help organize it. The sale was small, but very successful. Lots of actresses, their friends and our friends all came to sip chilled white wine, eat nibbles and buy, and we sold more than half our stock.

Shortly after this, El told me that her boyfriend, who lived and worked in Bristol, wanted her to come and live with him, and she had said yes. I was happy for her and sad for me.

A few weeks later, I went for my annual mammogram at the Princess Grace Hospital, after which I was told that they needed to do an ultrasound. I sat and waited, thinking that if men had to undergo mammograms, they would have invented a kinder way of doing them.

The results confirmed that I had breast cancer. I reacted with anger. Hadn't I had enough bloody surgery? There followed visits to various oncologist breast surgeons, and lots of scans, and I was forbidden to continue taking HRT. I had started taking it in my forties, when it was a lifesaver, but it seemed that being on it for 30 years might have given me breast cancer.

I decided that I couldn't carry on with Sarne. I put the wheels in motion to close it, and notified a friendly local commercial agent that the building was going to be for sale. Then I broke the news to Sherry and El. Sherry wasn't too unhappy, since it was a strain on her travelling from Brighton, and she had been offered freelance work putting new life into the well-established Clarks shoes brand. But El was in floods of tears – her boyfriend had changed his mind and ended their relationship. Sad as I was for her, I knew it really was time to stop. I was 72 years old and had breast cancer. How much energy, creativity and enthusiasm were going to be left in me after more surgery and goodness knows what else?

Before going into hospital, I decided to have a birthday dinner. I booked a big table at one of my favourite spots, upstairs at The Cow in Westbourne Park Road, a small restaurant above a very noisy pub owned by Tom Conran, whose ex-wife's house we had bought in London all those years ago.

Ted came with his wife, Willie; Ris with his husband, Rob; Sherry and her husband, Pablo; Janet Fischgrund, El, and Susannah Frankel, a journalist who had written wonderful articles about Ghost. They had all seen me through the highs and lows of my career and been there for me. It was a memorable evening, and although at times I felt tearful, I refrained from telling anyone my bad news. It was private.

My ample breasts had interfered with me being a ballet dancer when I was young, and a successful model when I was older, and had always got in the way of me looking elegant. But I was lucky. I only needed a lumpectomy on my left breast. I was spared the mastectomy, more often necessary for small breasts, my oncologist told me. For the first time in my life, I decided I loved my big bosoms. A couple of lymph nodes under my arm were also removed, but all in all it wasn't too much of an ordeal.

Post-operation, I had to do three weeks of radiotherapy. I was an old hand at this and sailed through it. The worst was to come, though. I had to block my female hormones and was told to take a nasty little pill every day for five years. From the day I took the first one, I have had several severe hot flushes every day and every night.

I returned to a forlorn El, who was minding the fort at Sarne HQ. An advertising company was interested in buying the building. Latimer Road was becoming very trendy by then; two buildings away from us was a famous rock star, and on the other side of the street, world-renowned photographer Juergen

Teller was constructing his studio. An old bus shelter a few buildings away had been turned into the Playground Theatre, and the Design Centre was also nearby. It was definitely a far more desirable location than it had been when we moved in.

The advertising people arrived en masse, and I was ignored while they poked into every corner of the premises. I wasn't keen on them. Shortly after they left, their boss phoned to say they 100 per cent wanted to buy the building, and please could he have my word that I wouldn't show it to anyone else. I replied that to have my word would cost him a 10 per cent deposit. He begged and pleaded, and finally we agreed that I wouldn't show it to anyone until his architect and stylist had inspected it. I told him he had one week.

Two days later, a group of people arrived. They discussed moving this and that, including my beautiful plants at the top of the staircase under the atrium. My antipathy to them grew. Later that day, the boss phoned me to reiterate that they wanted the building and on no account was I to show it to anyone else. I asked him if they just wanted it or were they going to buy it. My humour was lost on him. I asked for a deposit, and so did the agents. No deposit arrived.

A couple of weeks later, the charming gentleman who owned the twin half of our building happened to phone me about a mutual problem to do with lighting. As we chatted, I told him

I was going to retire and was selling my half of the building. He asked me how much it was on the market for. I told him, and added that it was as good as sold. He told me to unsell it; he would buy it for the same price. I agreed, and we exchanged the following week.

The advertising boss also phoned me that week to tell me he was sending in an electrician and plumber. I informed him that he wasn't sending in anyone; the building had been sold. Naturally he shouted and screamed at me. I didn't bother reminding him that I had waited four weeks for a deposit. There was no point, so I put the phone down.

El and I began the laborious task of moving everything to a little attic room in my house. I had once used this as my perfume-smelling room, after I was told by the perfumers that the best place to sample aromas is in the area under a gable roof where the walls form an A shape. When my perfume days ended, it had become Claudia's bedroom. Now it was just an attic used for storage.

On the floor beneath the attic was a very large room that we had made into a party room, with a bar and a pool table. This became our new office, as we still had a lot of loose ends to tie up. It is never simple closing a business, even a very tiny one. We set up two desks facing each other near the bar, where we put our kettle and mugs. There was a small fridge already installed behind the bar. We covered the pool table and set up rails either side of it for stock we had left. Filing cabinets and bookshelves came next. We decorated the walls with posters and pictures from Ghost, and we were ready to finish all the paperwork and then decide what to do with our lives.

I found a shop selling vintage clothes, which took a few pieces from me every week on a sale-or-return basis, which was a big help. We were left with a few precious pieces that were not for sale. Within a few months, that was it, Sarne was finished. I was delighted when the lovely El got a job as a designer for Penfield, and later on as head designer for men's accessories at Urban Outfitters.

There was only one area in the world of fashion or clothing that interested me. This was to try and restore Marks & Spencer to its former glory. When my great-aunt was alive, I had gone there to buy her the cashmere dressing gown she'd requested. It didn't exist. My daughter-in-law's mother had complained to me that she could no longer find a skirt in Marks that just covered her knees. I decided to do some research, and El came with me as I needed a second opinion.

We looked at hundreds of brassieres, none of which would have fitted me, or which I would have bought, and it was the same story with knickers. Back when Sheilagh had first asked me to provide some Ghost designs for M&S, she'd also asked my opinion of some of their ranges, including an underwear all-in-one that I told her fastened the wrong way round. I was amused to see that all these years later, it still did. All in all, we both agreed there was far too much choice and not enough quality.

I wrote a very studied letter to Stephen Rowe, the relatively new CEO. I told him I had grown up with Marks & Spencer when it was great, and that I would love to see it great again, which I didn't think would be that difficult if they were to supply the best quality basics available anywhere. I said I would love to help and would only accept renumeration based on results. I told him that my company, Ghost, had designed dresses and trousers for M&S that had sold brilliantly, that Alexandra Shulman, ex-editor of British *Vogue*, would give me a reference, and that I had received an OBE for my services to the fashion industry.

I don't know if Mr Rowe ever read my letter, but the reply I received several weeks later began: 'While we welcome comments from members of the public . . .'. I didn't know whether to laugh or cry. Suffice to say, that was that – my final interest in anything to do with fashion, dashed and gone.

Chapter Twenty

Reflections

———

Sarne was over. Done and dusted apart from all the invoices, which I had to keep for seven years. Wonderful, I thought. Now I can take it easy. It was 2018. I had set up my first business in 1978. Forty years of working in fashion surely justified my retirement. I settled down to contemplate my life, ignoring the mass of boxes, suitcases, files, clothes, fabrics, papers and photos surrounding me.

I found another reason for my retirement in my hot flushes. These were so severe that I was forced to stop whatever I was doing, sit or lie completely still and breathe deeply. No wonder I am grumpy as hell most days, though thankfully only in the mornings.

My being home every day changed life to some degree for Andrew, who had been used to me going out to work since we met, apart from my sabbatical year after Ghost. Although his studio was downstairs and my office was upstairs, he could still feel my presence, and it took a while for him to adjust. Lovely Andrew, who had been my sanity and stability throughout the turbulent years, putting up with my dramas and my moods.

When we first started seeing each other in 1991, we both enjoyed lots of fun and parties together. However, Andrew always preferred a clear head, liked running, and was keen to focus on his career, so he became teetotal very early on. Now we entered a new phase of our relationship, both living and working in the same house. And when we adjusted, we became even closer . . . affectionate, loving and caring.

We settled into a very happy pattern. At weekends we went to our house in the New Forest, but after a while, weekends turned into three days, and then four, and when the pandemic hit, we decided to stay there most of the time. Two tame hares live close by; we call them Jorge and Javier. There are too many deer to name. But we call our prancing, mincing pheasant Cock, because that's what he is. He feels he owns the place, loudly makes this clear to us every ten minutes, and protects a harem of hens hidden in the forest somewhere.

From our windows upstairs, or from the glass-fronted kitchen, we look out onto a forest that falls away from the house. We can see all the colours of the changing seasons. While working on this book, I marvelled at the hundreds of different shades of green. I feel incredibly lucky. Every day I wander through the forest talking to the trees, but I don't like the armies of bracken that invade in the summer. I call them triffids, like the monster plants in the novel *The Day of the Triffids* by John Wyndham.

Along with making programmes for the BBC, Andrew has become a woodsman, chopping up and drying wood to burn in our wood burners, planting trees and making our surroundings even more beautiful. We take our responsibility for the forest very seriously, and are careful not to disturb the wildlife. I wish the joy we feel in our home among the trees could go on for ever. Our nearest neighbour is a delightful lady in her eighties. She lives alone with her two dogs and has travelled the world. She is a descendant of the great 16th-century Irish female pirate Grace O'Malley, known as the Pirate Queen of Ireland, who had a turbulent relationship with Queen Elizabeth I. Some say O'Malley filled the Queen's coffers with silver and gold and supported her during the Nine Years War, which allowed her to continue being a pirate.

I thought I would have more time on my hands after I closed Sarne, but this was wishful thinking. Apart from seeing friends when I am in London, I shop for fresh food, cook lovely meals, play tennis, and regularly battle bureaucracy of one kind or another. Then there are the inevitable visits to the dentist, the optician, the endocrinologist, the knee and hip doctor, the breast clinic, the arthritis specialist, and my GP.

I do my best to stay healthy, but it's not easy getting old. As someone once said, old age ain't no place for sissies. It's all very well for people to claim it's all in the mind. It isn't. It's in the body and in the bones. Just like in any piece of machinery, the parts deteriorate. To keep everything working as best it can, I walk in the forest, play tennis and do exercises once a week with Graham Ferris, a wonderful expert in body and muscle strengthening. But I'm not a paragon of virtue, I love any excuse to stay in bed and play Sudoku.

I don't miss fashion one bit. It seems to me that the fun side of it has been replaced by corporate greed, and that all too often for independent businesses it has become a struggle to survive. I am so grateful that I was part of the fashion world at such an exciting, innovative time. I also marvel at how the wider world has changed since I was born, remembering fondly the excitement when the postman delivered letters instead of junk mail and bills, when a tablet was something you swallowed not wrote emails on, when you could stretch out your legs and look out of two windows travelling economy on an aeroplane, when you could watch a ballet or opera without people in the audience holding up iPhones to show off to their friends, when trainers were called plimsolls and were used only for sport and women mainly wore dresses. I wrote an article for an American magazine called *Flaunt* at the beginning of this century that still rings true.

So what's new? Or as the French say, *plus ça change, plus c'est la même chose* . . . The more they change, the more they stay the same!

The year 2000 is no different from the year 1900. One man dies from lack of clean water while another ponders over which coloured feathers he should use in his new hat creation. Old men with limp dicks get off by killing those who can do it, and politicians fabricate wars for their own ends. Tribesmen in deserts ride camels, while astronauts explore our universe in spacecraft. What a ridiculous world we live in and always will – given human nature. Having said this, I thank God I've spent over 50 years in the 20th century, rather than the 21st century.

I can communicate with people. I can cook with raw ingredients, play the piano, work out sales tax without a calculator, and my bottom hasn't spread from sitting in front of a computer screen for years. I've known the joy of driving on traffic-free roads with no speed limit. I've known the excitement of waiting for a phone call or letter and experienced the satisfaction of research well done without the help of the internet. I've known the delight of dressing up in glorious colours, crazy prints, glam lush velvets, geometric fantasies, beaded mini culottes, and the finest lace and silk macramé.

How boring and impersonal fashion has become. How much more simplistic and functional will it become? Few women have the luxury of dressing time or dressing maids, so minimal, instant dressing has become the norm. Black is unobtrusive, slimming and safe. Will fashion continue to be even more functional and less and less fun? Against my will and hopes, I have to say YES.

Innovation will come from technological developments, not artistic vision. It will come in the form of bulletproof, knife-proof, sweat-proof fabric. People's individuality will be increasingly suppressed as computerization empowers the state with greater and more accurate control. Cars won't start unless the driver proves to be alcohol free. Cars will stop if the driver exceeds the speed limit. Outdoor cameras will monitor our every movement, while video telephones record our physical presence. Who in this scenario would want to draw attention to themselves?

Only those who live in the past.

When I stop to reflect, I wonder what my life was all about. My first thought is that I have survived and given my family lineage through my children and grandchildren, after the horrors of the last world war and the murder of some of my family by the Nazis. It also brings me huge satisfaction to know that I gave pleasure to many women who found femininity and confidence through wearing my clothes. I am more than flattered by the Design Museum in London describing Ghost as 'one of those quiet revolutions where the significance of an event in fashion history goes almost unnoticed at first'.

I hope I have also given pleasure to people by helping and loving them. I don't think the Dalai Lama's vision of mankind – that most 'die having never really lived' – applies to me. I have lived. I have had an incredibly interesting and full life. I wonder sometimes if I could have done what I did if my mother had not died so young, or if I hadn't fuelled myself with alcohol, amphetamines and all sorts. I certainly would not have had the anger that also fuelled me. Maybe I would have had the energy, but I cannot imagine it now, as I feel my strength slipping away. I am told I need a new knee, a new hip, and the hand surgeon wants to take a bone out of my right thumb joint, which will render my hand useless for a few months. They all hurt, but I cannot face any more surgery right now, and in any case, I don't know which one to do first. I suppose a decision will be forced on me by circumstance.

Some people believe circumstance is God's will. I prefer to

think of it as the force of nature that inevitably leads one to take a particular route. Did I really have choices in my life? I'm not sure I did. I just followed my instinct. Maybe we have limited choices. This is a discussion I will leave to my grandson, who is studying philosophy.

I used to dream of travelling when I gave up work. I had visions of roaming across India over several months. Ever since I read James A Michener's *Caravans* in my teens, I have wanted to go to the Khyber Pass. Now that is impossible, since men seem determined to throw away their lives fighting and dying – over what? How stupid, how wasteful, how horrible. I will be content with having seen the Danube Delta, and the glaciers and snowy mountains of Switzerland before they melt away. I have also seen parts of Mexico, Brazil, the USA, North Africa, Jamaica, Bali, and most of the countries of Europe. And that is enough. As my darling Granny Ekee used to say, I've seen enough of the world.

Now I like my home comforts, and in our beautiful New Forest home we have just been privileged to watch the forest emerge from its winter slumbers and come alive in spring. I am so fortunate. Not only have I witnessed nature in all its beauty during the months of pandemic lockdown, I have the most wonderful husband to share it all with. My two incredibly loving children are both in very happy marriages, and between them they have produced five beautiful grandchildren whom I adore. Saul, who I spent so much time with when I was asked to leave Ghost, is now 19 and a student at Oxford University, Lucius and Isiah are both 15 and approaching manhood, and Ione and Azura are 11 and on the cusp of being teenagers. All of them mean so much to me, and I am grateful every single day for their presence in my life.

I would like to be able to communicate much better with my grandchildren, and with young people in general, but our points of reference are so different. The TV, films and computer games they love are a mystery to me, in the same way that what I love mystifies them. If I talk about one of my favourite films, *On the Waterfront*, virtually no one under the age of 60 has heard of it, or of *The Red Shoes*, starring Moira Shearer, another one of my all-time favourites. They have never heard of Charlton Heston, Marlene Dietrich, Humphrey Bogart or even Clark Gable. But while our cultural differences are many, what matters most is that I adore them and the way that each of them is unique. Watching them grow towards adulthood is a joy.

I treasure old friends, too. Gina Newson, who was one of my few friends at school; Chrissy Iley, who went from being my best customer at Ghost to becoming a true friend; Ris, Sherry and El, my work companions. I am so glad that they continue to be a part of my life. And Michael, infuriating and delightful in equal measure, is also now an old friend who I enjoy meeting for dinner with one or other – or sometimes several – of our children and grandchildren.

If I have a wish, it is to grow old gracefully. So many old people I have met in my life, including my father and his mother, were bitter, bad-tempered and unpleasant. I understand why. They are in a lot of discomfort, they find themselves slow and struggling to understand what is going on. They see young people having fun running around and all they can feel is their bones aching. I understand, but I don't intend to join them. I am determined to keep smiling, no matter what.

And singing too. I hear music in my head, but it just doesn't come out the way I want it to, so I have started having singing lessons with an excellent teacher called Sarah Stanton. She has promised me I will, in time, be able to sing a whole song like a proper singer, but I'd better hurry up. Who knows what's round the corner?

My one great fear is of losing my independence. I can still do the dog and tree positions in yoga, but my balance is getting worse, and I have to sit down to put my jeans on. Despite my arthritis, I can still play the piano. I love shopping for good food, cooking and driving. I never want to have to ask someone else to do these things for me, not even my husband, who I love and adore. I want to be able to walk in the sunshine and walk in the rain and make my own bed. As the saying goes, 'life's a bitch and then you die'. To hell with the aches and pains, to hell with my wearing and tearing bones, I will enjoy the rest of my life, and as the Leiber and Stoller song 'Is That All There Is?', so movingly sung by Peggy Lee, goes . . .

> If that's all there is, my friends,
> Then let's keep dancing
> Let's break out the booze and have a ball,
> If that's all . . . there . . . is.

PS But maybe not the booze.

Index

Index

Acknowledgements

A very special thank you to the following:

Karl Plewka, who inspired me to write this book, gave it its title and interviewed many people to help me remember.

Caro Handley, who brilliantly structured my endless ramblings.

My husband, Andrew, without whose technical and literary help I wouldn't have got here.

I would also like to thank all the people interviewed for the book who helped me remember the past through their many lovely and insightful observations: Alex Barlow, Amy Roberts, Angela Southwell, Chrissy Iley, Debbi Mason, El Sheriff, Francis Ryan, Janet Fischgrund, Katrina Phillips, Lynne Franks, Mary Greenwell, Ris Fatah, Sam McKnight, Sherald Lamden, Sophia Malig, Ted Walters, Vicki Sarge and Iain R. Webb.